PERSONAL MASTERY

COMPETENCE-BEHAVIOUR FRAMEWORKS

C Bhaktavatsala Rao

LEADERCREST ACADEMY

INDIA • SINGAPORE • MALAYSIA

ISBN 979-8-89133-359-8

Contents

List of Figures

Other Books by the Author

From Start-up to Ramp up: Indian Context and Global Insights

Technology and Competitive Strategy: Strategies for Innovators, Differentiators and Followers

Competitive Strategy: A Contemporary Retake

Leadership for India Inc.: An Experiential Treatise

India as Global Start-up Hub: Mission with Passion

India's Economic Resurgence: A Modified Paradigm for a Welfare State

Work-Life Balance: Essays in Individual and Organizational Behaviour

Product Strategy and Corporate Success: Concepts and Cases from the Indian Automobile Industry

Strategic Management: Practice and Philosophy for India Inc.

STEM: Strategy. Technology. Entrepreneurship. Management

Legendary Leaders: Insights and Lessons

Dharmic Management: Lessons from the Indian Social Ecosystem

Strategic Marketing: Cases and Concepts from the Indian Business

Foreword

Every individual has characteristics that comprise capabilities, aptitudes, attitudes, emotions, and aspirations, among others. These characteristics continuously evolve in a person. These, in a sense, are expressions of the energy of a person. Only when these are developed in a positive manner, with mutual alignment, would an individual feel fulfilled. Given that every individual is a part of multiple ecosystems, from the family to the organization, each with its own changing dynamics, the fulfilment does not come easy. Personal mastery helps a person achieve that fulfilment.

This book titled 'Personal Mastery: Competence–Behaviour Frameworks' aims to lead the readers on a journey of personal mastery. Life provides to an individual as many opportunities as challenges. An awareness of what one is and what one can be is the key to embarking on a journey of personal progress. This journey must involve a deep appreciation of the ecosystem dynamics and a determined effort to achieve personal mastery.

Personal mastery, and not educational degree or organizational title, must be the critical aspiration of every person. It involves setting and achieving high standards of performance, with positive contributions to the family, the organization, and the society. The journey is a journey of introspection, reflection, and betterment. It involves self-awareness, self-motivation, self-discipline, self-confidence, and self-control, besides inter-personal relationships. Personal mastery involves building strong competencies and positive behaviours. This book presents multiple frameworks to achieve personal mastery.

This book comprises thirty chapters; in contrast to my approach with my other books, I have chosen not to straitjacket them into thematic sections. Each chapter presents an independent yet interconnected framework. One may benefit by focusing on a few approaches only to start with and eventually seek mastery over all the constructs and frameworks outlined. Personal mastery is a dynamic lifelong journey of continuous improvement. One should feel free to pace this journey as a journey of self-actualization.

Personal mastery is not necessarily aimed at becoming more competitive or establishing superiority. It is also not about rewards and recognitions. It just involves becoming what one is capable of becoming, by understanding oneself and others better. The key to personal mastery lies in raising the bar of self-actualization continuously. The benchmark of personal mastery, therefore, lies within oneself.

As always, I will be open for readers' feedback. I can be reached at cbrao2005@gmail.com.

With best wishes and warm regards

C Bhaktavatsala Rao
Chennai
September 01, 2023

Chapter 1

Aspiration, Balance, Competence, and Achievement

Aspiration and achievement are the two ends of a journey that need to be bridged consistently for one to feel fulfilled. Aspiration, which is a natural human tendency, has become an organizational characteristic too given that organizations are mere conglomerations of human beings. Aspiration itself varies significantly across human beings as much as it does between organizations. Broadly, however, positive facets such as knowledge, experience, growth, income, sustainability, and responsible citizenship mark the aspiration mix, whether of an individual or an organization. Each of the facets, of course, is defined by one or more metrics such as educational degrees, career span, professional status, pay, income and savings, social recognition, and goodwill for an individual. Corporations also are judged on these facets by intellectual property, longevity, business rank, revenue, profitability and net worth, brand image, and corporate citizenship.

The array of metrics points to the challenges inherent in converting an aspiration into an achievement. The journey from aspiration to achievement can be casual or confident and fulfilling or disappointing, depending on how insightfully the goals are set and how confidently one traverses the path from aspiration to achievement. The path from aspiration to achievement is rarely linear; external opportunities and challenges as well as internal competencies and deficiencies determine the relative ease and arduousness of the journey. One must strike the right balance between staying laser-focused on originally set goals and adapting them contextually on a real-time basis. This is the key aspect of achieving one's full potential without undue stress or inappropriate laxity. There are four fundamental aspects that drive this process, namely, aspiration, balance, competence, and diligence. These are factors that are individually relevant but become even more powerful when paired. This chapter develops a paradigm of aspirational balance and competent diligence as a guidepost to sustainable success.

Aspiration, Competence, Balance, and Diligence

Aspiration is a strong desire to achieve something. Aspiration usually has a strong emotive driver, sometimes accompanied by inherent biases. Without aspiration, exceptional progress becomes impossible for individuals, organizations, and nations. Rags to Riches, Man on Moon, Rover on Mars, India in Space Club, Polio-free World, Vaccines for Cancer, Regenerative Medicine, Personalized Medicine, Self-driving Automobiles, Clean Energy, and Space Tourism are some aspirations that may have looked impossible at the time of their formulation but eventually have become or are becoming realizable. Aspiration needs competence to enable performance. Studious and intellectual individuals as well as knowledge corporations and economies have deliberately focused on competence building as the foundational means to enable performance and fulfil aspirations. Aspiration and competence form a virtuous cycle, with each prompting the other to higher levels. However, the virtuous cycle is reinforced or eroded by the embedded behavioural balance and diligence, respectively.

Balance is the intrinsic quality of an individual (or entity) to appreciate his or her (its) own strengths and weaknesses, or own highs and lows, and set himself or herself (itself) for success. It is an internal compass that is fine-tuned continuously with learning and development. Balance arises from a high level of sensitivity to facts and figures as well as insights and feelings, without any biases. Balance helps one overcome one's weaknesses and reinforce one's strengths. Diligence reflects an approach to work that is marked by focus, care, and effort. Diligence involves a strong application of knowledge and experience to new problems. Aspiration requires that one should convert impossibilities into possibilities, and possibilities into realizations. In this process, competence provides the wherewithal to achieve the goals. Balance helps one choose the right aspirational goals while diligence makes the seemingly impossible eventually possible. Aspirational balance and competent diligence make the winning pairs for success. At various levels, from micro-local to mega-global, one can cite innumerable examples of aspirational balance and competent diligence leading to exceptional achievements. Figure 1.1 gives a summary of aspiration, competence, balance, and diligence.

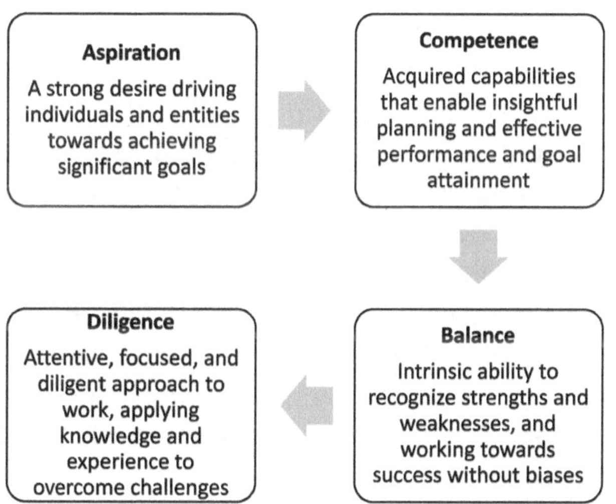

Figure 1.1: Aspiration, Competence, Balance, and Diligence

Tightrope Walking

The interplay of the four factors is best illustrated by tightrope walking. Aspiration and balance are interlinked and interrelated as goal and moderator respectively, but the subtlety of their constitution and the complexity of their interaction are not well understood. Aspiration is a desire tinged with ambition of achieving something which is not readily achievable. Balance is the art of staying stable, managing two extremes of anything. Aspiration is imitable while balance is inimitable. To amplify a little more, the human brain is naturally wired to seek satiation (through aspiration that comes out of social existence) but needs enormous exertion to achieve it (through balance that is enabled by individual effort).

Aspiration is a social influence while balance is individual discrimination. Balance can be misunderstood as a limit to development; on the other hand, it is an enabler to move to higher trajectories. The case of the tightrope walker is a perfect example of balance being an integral part of aspiration, serving as an internal compass and perfecting itself through learning and development. Tightrope walking is not everyone's cup of tea; while everyone is a natural walker, only very few are natural tightrope walkers. Competence to be a tightrope walker comes with training but stays only with diligence. The tightrope walker cannot afford to miss even a second in applying his or her competence; that is where diligence counts. Competence through education is knowledge while through practice is skill. Diligence that comes with discipline is practical while that comes with ownership is insightful. Competence is visible and quantifiable while diligence is invisible and embedded. Human faculties respond both appropriately and inappropriately to various triggers. Aspiration can inspire achievement, when appropriate. When brazenly overestimated, aspiration could be unsettling. Deft balancing understands risk and reward objectively. Skewed understanding of risk and reward leads to imbalance. Ever-vigilant competence leads to success while resting on oars too soon blunts competition. Optimal diligence improves insights while sub-optimal diligence or excessive diligence obfuscates the real issues. The perfection with which an individual (or an entity) integrates aspiration, competence, balance, and diligence defines sustainable success.

Influencers

Aspiration can be related to competence, balance, and diligence. If aspiration and competence are seen as the two dimensions of a 2x2 matrix, individuals can fall into one of the four grids: Low Aspiration – Low Competence (LALC), High Aspiration – Low Competence (HALC), Low Aspiration – High Competence (LAHC), and High Aspiration – High Competence (HAHC). As demonstrated in Figure 1.2, HAHC individuals are Masters of their own destiny. LALC individuals are Losers. HALC individuals are unrealistic Daydreamers. All individuals must strive to move into the HAHC Mastery grid.

To supplement this, the Competence dimension can be replaced by Balance dimension or Diligence dimension. Individuals need to be high on Aspiration and high on Balance to complement Mastery. Losers would be baulking and failing at all opportunities, whereas Masters would be Achievers, setting highly competitive barriers for others. Daydreamers would be low on Balance and Diligence while for Laggards, high Balance and high Diligence would be of no avail. These classifications need not necessarily stay constant and consistent throughout the lifespans of individuals or entities. Awareness (or lack of it) determines the entry and mobility drivers across the four quadrants.

Given that careers and corporate longevity are like marathon races, a high level of awareness on Aspiration–Competence–Balance–Diligence interplay is required for optimizing the Aspiration–Balance grid. It is self-evident that Losers, Laggards and Daydreamers must make conscious efforts to build competencies and inspire themselves to be balanced and diligent. On the other hand, Masters would be winning all-round appreciation for their perfect synergy of capability and application.

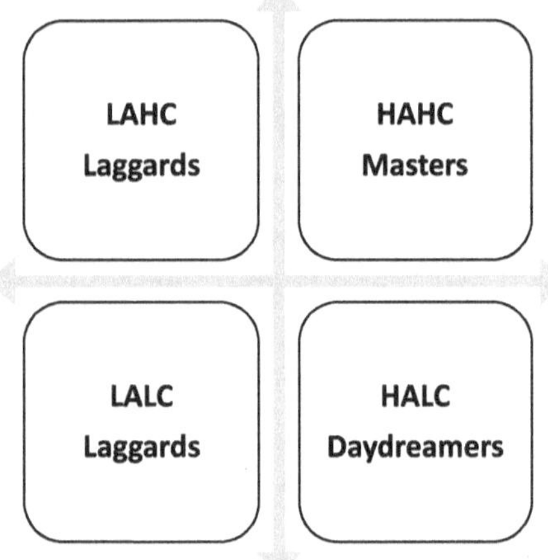

Figure 1.2: The Four Quadrants of the Aspiration – Competence Grid

World is a Circus

We have seen tightrope walking as an example of how aspiration, competence, balance, and diligence are required to perform and deliver beyond what a human body and mind is biologically and naturally accustomed to. On a broader canvas, the world is so competitive and volatile that one needs to be all that a consummate circus artist needs to be, whether a tightrope walker, trapeze artist, gymnast, acrobat, juggler, or even joker. In a circus show, the performers are few and applauders are many. In the real world, which is a circus of high performance of multiple talents, everyone is expected to be a performer. Consummate artistry in the chosen dimension of talent is inescapable to stay successful. As with a circus artist, maintaining the equilibrium while defying gravity is an essential requirement for a contemporary individual or entity.

Given that career progression and corporate longevity are like marathon races, a high level of awareness and a high level of focus on the four determinants of success, namely aspiration, competence, balance, and diligence constitute the essential foundations of consummate artistry. Whether one would be a loser, laggard or daydreamer or a masterly achiever would entirely depend on how one sets about developing one's own gravity-defying equilibristic capabilities. Successful artistes are those who learnt the performance artistry from the very young age and sustained it throughout the lifespan. For very fortunate few, world may be a ready-made canvas on which they can paint a picture of choice. For most, however, world is a circus of competitive performing artists where nothing less than consummate artistry gets the applause.

Chapter 2

From Jobs to Careers

Job fulfilment is the precursor for job satisfaction. Given that more than 50% of a 24-hour day and more than 80% of the wakeful part is spent on the job or job-related activities, job satisfaction is necessary for peace in life. Deriving fulfilment on the job is essential for peace in life, therefore. Job fulfilment cannot be defined in terms of either title or compensation. It is more in terms of doing what one enjoys and what one's natural aptitudes and talents play for, and finally the impact one makes through one's job on the people and organization. In some cases, job fulfilment occurs immediately upon joining work while in some cases it takes years to happen. In most cases, what was fulfilment at the start gets overwhelmed by greater accomplishments later in life but in some cases, the later day's greater successes owe much to the initial fulfilments, and consequent inspirations too.

For a teacher, for example, job fulfilment occurs when he or she can coach his class to high scores in examinations. The real job fulfilment, however, comes when the teacher sees her students occupying high positions and becoming successful in life. The teacher, in the process, starts getting more fulfilled from the teaching process, with the long-term implications of students getting high scores, and their bringing credit to the teacher and the alma mater in the years to come. Today's competitive landscape pressurizes the executives for immediate performance, much like examination results, and ingrains a mindset of seeking immediate fulfilment through rewards and recognitions. While there is nothing commercially wrong in this (except for the accumulation of stress), the flip side is that executives, no longer, can await and relish the long-term results from the seeds they sow.

Jobs Make Careers

Most advertisements for recruitment or placement agency communications no longer emphasize the job; they speak of career. Most recruiters emphasize how career can be built up by the prospective candidates through the position under call. More fundamental, however, is the definition of the role. A company that lays emphasis on talent mapping and succession planning can, indeed, assure a fulfilling career through a proper definition of the role that the executive is expected to play. Such companies are characterized by their frontline executives growing to occupy CXO positions eventually. It is, therefore, unnecessary, and even misplaced to distinguish between jobs or roles and careers. If jobs make careers for individuals, and both mean fulfilment for them, it is important to realize that companies also have their own jobs and careers to fulfil for the society. In fact, it is only within the aegis of a company that individuals can find fulfilment.

While individuals can find jobs in any company, successful or not so successful, they can find careers only in successful companies. They can, however, shape their own careers in not-so-successful companies as well by transforming them into successful companies with their jobs. Like an individual, a company has also a job to do in terms of delivering the products and services. However, the company also has an evolutionary journey to make, in terms of maintaining a continuity of products and services that are ever more beneficial to the customer. Just as an individual gets to change jobs in search of fulfilment or career, companies also get to churn their products and services (and even employees) in their quest for existential fulfilment in the business landscape. While these similarities are easy to appreciate, the interplay between jobs and careers as well as between individuals and companies (in permutations and combinations thereof) is not understood by either the individuals or the companies. Perceptive business leaders and HR leaders not only appreciate this interplay but work in partnership to address this complex issue. Figure 2.1 presents the circle of career growth that encompasses individual and company responsibilities. Role definition, job performance and career development constitute the triad of individual fulfilment with positive effect on organizational growth.

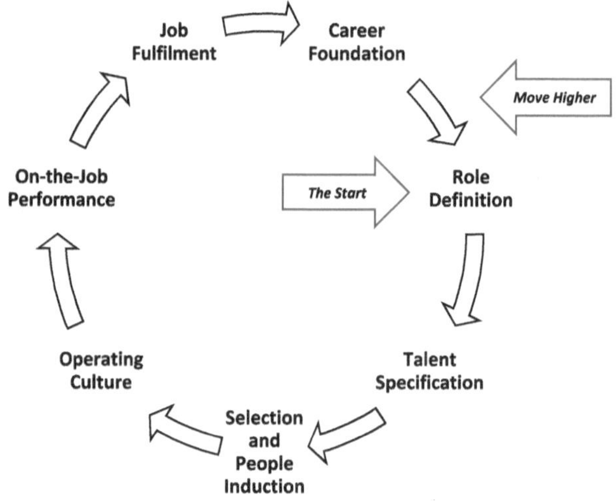

Figure 2.1: The Circle of Career Growth

Defining Fulfilment

Many people perceive and seek fulfilment in terms of how their talents impact the jobs that they carry out. One is apt to make statements such as "I completed my assigned project that was appreciated by my boss" or "I made a presentation that the audience liked." Fulfilment through such feelings and perceptions is misplaced. True fulfilment occurs when the job impacts positively and meaningfully others in the organization, and one feels invested in the company's future through the job one is performing. Again, it is not a matter how many people one leads but it does matter how much interaction one is able to have with other relevant internal and external stakeholders. True fulfilment also occurs when one can experience, on a first-hand basis, the results of one's work. Typically, jobs (especially in mature established organizations) tend to stay static while talent that is available to meet the roles (as defined by a combination of education and experience) may become surplus.

Fulfilment becomes elusive when jobs trail competencies. There would also be cases when jobs (especially in turnaround situations or sunrise industries) require new skills while talents (as required by new requirements) remain static. In this case also, where skills trail job challenges, fulfilment becomes elusive. Fulfilment, overall, is a dynamic concept that can work only when jobs or roles, as they are designed, staffed, and performed, lead to the growth of businesses. This is not merely a HR responsibility but the responsibility of the entire leadership team of a company at one level. It is also, more importantly, the responsibility of the individuals themselves at another level.

Economic View

It is impossible to discuss job fulfilment without considering an economic viewpoint. Typically, companies extract consumer surplus when they market their products or services at prices higher than costs. Consumer surplus obviously varies based on the product-market segments. In a similar fashion, companies seek to benefit from employee surplus by deriving higher value from their services than the salaries paid to them. The laws of growth and competition not only legitimize the relevance of consumer surplus and employee surplus but also seek to reduce consumer surplus and employee surplus. Companies try to counter this by maximizing employee surplus, but this may not always be feasible in a skill-scarce and talent-constrained economy.

This riddle of economic fulfilment can only be resolved through sustainable and profitable growth. The economics of fulfilment for individuals, in their twin roles as customers and employees, and for companies, in their multiple roles as producers and sellers, and as employers and optimizers are important. Growth economics, in fact, is a bubble. Population demographics is a reality. The bubble must be sustained to meet the reality. Unless economic growth stays continuous and consistent, social fulfilment becomes elusive. When viewed in this perspective, job fulfilment can never be a matter of individual joy or disappointment, and not even of role design and talent deployment. It is a matter of finding business and economic solutions for challenges of growth. Job fulfilment occurs when the role of an individual is appreciated by the role designers, and the individual can appreciate the role as part of a larger socioeconomic paradigm.

Cruise or Exploration?

When this socioeconomic perspective is understood, frontline executives as well as their employers start assessing objectively whether job fulfilment is a matter of immediacy and surety as a highway cruise is or is a matter of uncertainty with sporadic abundance as oil exploration is. The answer is rather simple. The concept of a career highway, however desirable, is rather a desire than reality in organizations. There are far too many variables in the process of interactions of individual–business–environment that there can never be a preset path. It is unclear, for example, if the conventional synthetic medicines will be dominant a decade hence or biologic medicines or genetic engineering would be dominant. Taking the example of automobile industry, the future automobile could be a digital machine. Career highways based on current business models and current skill sets could be misleading.

On the other hand, job fulfilment is more like oil exploration. Not every field, whether onshore or offshore, offers potential for oil, and not every field with potential for oil ends up providing an unending gush of oil. Job fulfilment for aspirant executives arises from a process of identifying the right companies and persevering with their job roles and career paths with grit. As with oil exploration, the operating circumstances tend to be challenging but when the right role is struck, the rewards could be plenty. Like oil exploration, exploration of job fulfilment tends to be a combination of hardware, soft skills, and the entire organization working together. While the simile may seem extended, the underlying concept that job fulfilment is a larger enterprise-wide challenge is a reality. Does the individual have an easy path then? Figure 2.2 brings out a comparison of the highway cruise and oil exploration models of the job fulfilment journey.

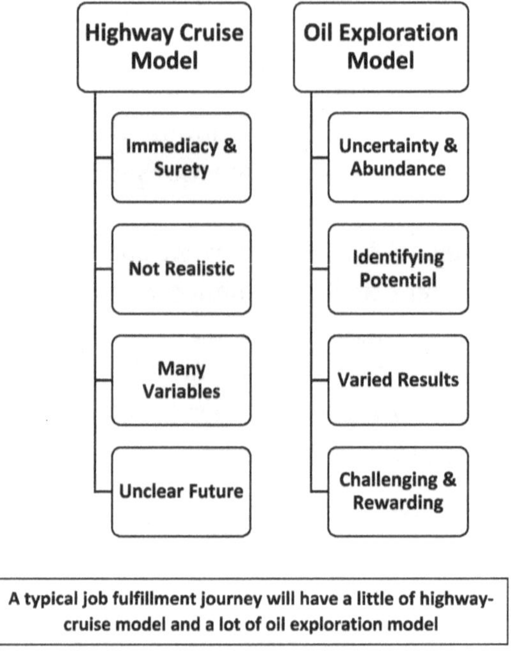

Figure 2.2: Job Fulfillment Model

Aligned Fulfilment

The solution for job fulfilment lies in aligned fulfilment between the company and the employees. The company must have a larger purpose and mission that must have the buy-in of the employees. The company and the employee must have a clear view of how the dynamics of industrial competition would impact the economics of consumer surplus and economic surplus. Just as the company feels justified in deriving a consumer surplus based on the perceived value of its products and services to the company, the employee must feel a broader purpose in providing the employee surplus to the company. A good job for a competent person pays well. A great job that is derived from a sense of purpose for the company and covers its employees inclusively leads to fulfilment for them as well as the company.

Chapter 3

Employee Creativity

Employee creativity is essential for the growth of corporations or for that matter any organization, be it in public sector or private sector. It is interesting how start-ups are fired up by creative energy while large corporations struggle to retain creative energy. Even highly creative firms such as Microsoft and Google, which are founded solely on creativity, have been facing the burden of largeness affecting their basic DNA of creativity. It is not unusual, therefore, for large organizations, for example Procter & Gamble and 3M, to devise ways and means to retain their creative energy despite the size. The models adopted by such firms are usually structure-, process-, or initiative-driven, and despite their relative success do not represent a universal model of employee and organizational creativity. Some of the approaches of creative firms focus on the pursuit of open innovation (embracing ideas from outside the organization), percolation of strategic thinking down the organization (enabling strategy deployment at unit or department level) and relying on technology to drive innovation (letting products create markets).

These approaches, however, occur in phases with creativity going through cyclical downturns, often influenced by strategic shifts and lapses. Nothing else, for example, explains how a leader in televisions in the 1980s like Sony (with its famous Trinitron picture tubes) completely lost ground to Samsung and the likes that revolutionized the television industry in the 2000s with flat panel displays. More striking is the case of Nokia, a pioneer in mobile phone devices, losing the position completely due to its persistence with non-competitive operating systems. Only those organizations that institutionalize creativity at the employee level may hope to always remain competitive. Creativity is the ability of an individual to visualize imaginatively, think innovatively, and act effectively to achieve an end-result with value-adding differentiation. Creativity also signifies an ability to overcome known and unknown challenges with the least possible expenditure of additional resources.

Creativity is significantly different from pursuit of excellence. When limits to excellence begin to operate, only creativity and innovation can take companies to different trajectories. In a competitive and uncertain world, companies that are creative would most certainly have advantage over companies that are not. Nevertheless, creativity figures low in corporate agenda as a work or organizational ethic that needs to be institutionalized. For most organizations, only the visible working of an employee mind to follow the prescribed practices is relevant. The employee mind is considered akin to a black box ("one can never fathom what happens inside a human brain, nor is it necessary")! For most organizations, their environmental view rarely strays beyond an explored business canvas into unexplored white spaces ("one has to have deep pockets to lose money on white spaces")! By failing to dip into the thought processes that go through the black boxes, companies miss on the opportunities of white-space growth that lies ahead of them.

Creativity–Conformity Conundrum

Organizations are often faced with a creativity–conformity conundrum that needs to be optimally resolved to ensure both differentiation and focus simultaneously. Organizations are nothing but aggregations of heterogeneous people who are brought together to achieve a common purpose, complying with certain organizational ethos and norms. Implicit in this is the need for organizations to be homogeneous in the way they think, talk, and act. Conformity to the organizational processes and systems as well as corporate goals and strategies is essential for organizations to achieve oneness despite individual plurality. On the other hand, creativity is a trait that requires freedom of thinking and action. Creativity gets institutionalized in organizations when individuals are enabled freedom of thought, communication, and execution. Creativity requires reinforcement through acceptance and execution of ideas, which in turn calls for expenditure of resources. In one sense, conformity enables organizational focus with frugality while creativity sparks corporate differentiation at the risk of profligacy. Competitive dynamics of a business are often difficult to navigate. They mandate focus and specialization, and demand differentiation and diversification simultaneously.

While large firms and conglomerates are probably better placed to cater to the apparently conflicting needs, small and medium firms find the demands of competitive dynamics extremely complex to resolve. This is where creativity as a corporate strategy and as an organizational ethic comes in handy. Contrary to popular perception, creativity does not ipso facto lead to profligacy. Some creative ideas may require resources to implement, and some may lead to multiple foci; but some may neither need additional resources nor create additional streams of work. Creativity could often find a better way to accomplish the set strategies, more productively and more effectively, and could many times lead to breakthrough strategies, to catapult companies into new trajectories. It is, therefore, important that organizations understand the conformity–creativity conundrum more perceptively and create an optimal balance, and synergy, between the two essential sources of competitive advantage. In organizations, conformity needs systemic strength to be effective while creativity needs cultural enablement to flourish.

Conformity supports better execution, which requires clearly defined projects, programs, systems, and processes. In the absence of these systemic enablers, conformity becomes individualized to boss–subordinate relationships, often leading to multiple and often conflicting approaches across the organization. Creativity supports better planning, which requires ideation to develop alternatives and evaluate vision, strategy, and performance vis-à-vis aspirations from time to time. In the absence of these strategy enablers, pursuit of creativity becomes a purposeless diffusion of organizational effort. Prudent and dynamic organizations resolve this conundrum by establishing the core foundations of business discipline while cantilevering the core to enhance business efficiency and achieve business diversity. To be able to do that, however, organizations need to disparage their mindsets of the perception that creativity is all about strategy, and hence is the responsibility of the corporate elite. Creativity is a competence and a great enabler for the broader organizational team even if the team's main responsibility is to execute. Figure 3.1 illustrates the creativity–conformity conundrum.

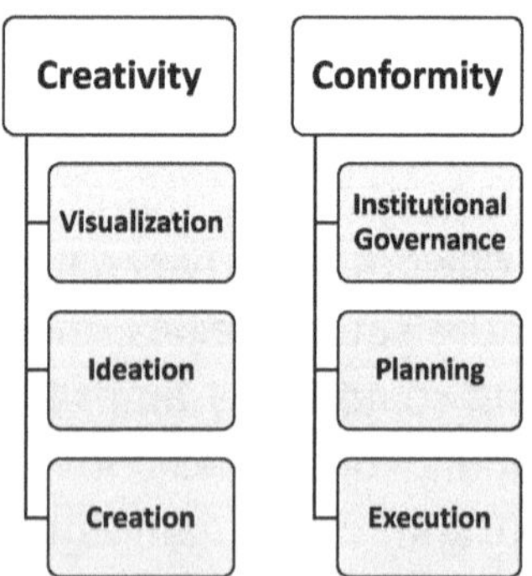

Figure 3.1: The Creativity–Conformity Conundrum

Manifestations of Creativity

Creativity is not all about corporate vision or strategy. Creativity, on the other hand, is the core of on-ground continuous improvements as well as the launchpad of breakthrough developments. Creativity improves existing products as much as it generates new ones. Creativity enables new manufacturing processes as much as it enhances the capability of existing processes. Creativity enables market segmentation as much as it creates new user needs. Creativity extends to every function of an organization and may never be limited to only innovation in research. Creativity results in product superiority as much as it leads to cost competitiveness. Creativity seeds and grows new businesses as much as it protects and extends existing businesses. Creativity makes industries more resilient and self-reliant even as it connects and even amalgamates multiple industries into one whole new industry. Creativity happens at the leadership level as much as at the frontline worker level.

Creativity is pervasive and universal in its concept, execution, and ownership. In everyday life, we encounter occurrences that demonstrate how creativity achieves all the above. There was, not so long ago, a time when the USB data cable and charger were separate and distinct accessories in a smart device. Subsequently, simple standardization with USB at one end and micro-USB at the other end merged both the accessories into a single-cable unit. This is an example of how simple creativity could lead to cost savings through continuous improvement. On the other hand, when a detachable tablet computer is configured to morph into a netbook computer, enabling dual use as a tablet and netbook based on needs, it represents a complex improvement, capable of creating a new market segment. However, if a palm-held computer that would read the electrical signals of the brain and other parameters of the body as an individual conducts his or her day-to-day affairs is developed, it would represent a breakthrough innovation that redefines life and creates new markets. Contemporaneously, the full-screen foldable cell phone technology can be innovatively reverse-engineered to develop a new generation of full-screen laptops.

Successful and creative transplantation of technologies from one industry to another would result in product innovations that could be game changers. If the roof and side panels of cars are also solar panels a new hybrid car revolution could take place, for example. If the kinetic energy of a mobile phone in a walking person's hand or pocket is converted into chargeable electric energy (as in the case of watches), it would represent a typical technology redeployment. Vintage machine tools could achieve enhanced performance with superior jigs and fixtures as well as stronger tools and dies. Sequential machine tools could be amalgamated into machining centres and reconfigured into flexible manufacturing systems with creativity.

When conventional metal cutting is replaced by laser cutting or when a surgeon's scalpel is replaced by a laser beam, it is creativity of transplantation. Additive manufacture or 3D printing is a transformational approach to accomplish precise, flexible, and no-waste manufacturing. Yet, successful transplantation is not a result of any one singular technology. Biological-engineering interfaces on one hand and hardware–software integrations on the other reflect the need for multiple functions and domains to collaborate to make creative improvements and breakthroughs feasible. The few examples given here may give the impression that creativity and complexity go hand in hand. Harnessing of fundamental research and use of several technologies, some of them unrelated, indicates that creativity requires higher-order abilities. On the other hand, creativity is multi-layered, the first layer of which is simple and spontaneous ideation.

Ideation, the Engine of Creativity

Creativity at the core is just ideation. From Newton to Archimedes, simple observations resulted in groundbreaking laws, whereas from Bell to Edison, fulfilment of day-to-day needs resulted in breakthrough products. In the bygone era of limited education and constrained industrialization, it was left to the passion and brilliance of individual scientists to be creative. In today's context of broad-based education and unfettered industrialization, creativity could be everyone's cup of tea. More particularly, if simple ideation is seen to be the engine of complex creativity, there is no reason why every employee in an organization, or for that every individual in the society, cannot participate in a revolution of ideation.

Japanese companies have long realized this vital trend and made kaizen or continuous improvement, through creative grassroots ideas, the fountainhead of performance enhancement. The same has been the case with the Japanese concept of quality circles. There is no need for any other proof that ideation is in everyone's realm. Ideation to work in organizations needs two triggers: challenge and motivation. Employees need to be challenged to find improvements to everyday issues. The challenge is that no human endeavour, even with the best of technology, is perfect; there would always be room for improvement. Even as new products are conceived leading to improved need fulfilment, the quest for perfection only increases. Designers, manufacturers, and marketers need to be constantly challenged to update their own creations.

It is established that a product in today's environment undergoes at least two upgrades every year, and potentially goes through at least few annual generations before it is completely overshadowed by a new breakthrough product. Innovative firms have laboratories that seek ideation from every source – for example, sales and service reports, competitor products, vendor experiences, shop-floor feedback, and employee opinions, and convert the prioritized ideas into product actions. Only a few companies realize the power of having all their employees thinking about process improvement all the time. At Toyota, each year, every employee generates on average at least ten ideas, aggregating in the process several thousands, and even a million of improvement ideas. Each of these ideas enhances efficiency and saves money. Over 99% of the ideas are reportedly implemented. Ideation is sustained and reinforced by the motivational culture of a company. Contrary to perceptions, financial incentives are not the sole instruments of motivation; in fact, in many cases they could fail to motivate too. The reason is that ideation is a spontaneous response to an individual's yearning for self-actualization. The greatest satisfaction an employee or a team derives from ideation is to see the ideas blossom into physical improvements.

When I visited the Toyota plant in Nagoya, Japan, in the early 1990s, I found the factory operations to be an object lesson in continuous ideation. A quietly efficient Toyota factory is characterized by the highly synchronized coordination of the arrival and assembly of the 30,000 parts of an automobile, the minute-by-minute completion of the automobile assembly that is perfectly balanced to Takt Time, the visual signals that are prominent everywhere, and the error-proofing of manufacture as well as the supportive component and subassembly movement. The nuances of the Toyota Production System are so subtle and effective that only an underlying credo of spontaneous and continuous ideation can support such a hugely successful innovative machine. The large sign that is in both Japanese and English, announcing "Good Thinking, Good Products" in a Toyota plant brings out the motivational impact. Toyota values the creative energy of its employees by tying up the duties of supervision and management to the generation of improvement ideas by the workers. When one looks at Toyota's record of financial performance over the last several decades, and the evidence of employees' creative ideas to power this performance, there is clearly a lesson here for all businesses and all organizations.

Arithmetical Potential of Ideation

For committed and talented employees, work just grows on them, day over day. For those who spend a lifetime on their jobs, ideas constantly flow through the mind rather subconsciously. Yet, managers and leaders fail to harness the potential due to three commonly held fallacies. Firstly, it is rarely understood that creative ideas come up spontaneously to only the uninhibited employees. Creative expression needs to be facilitated in those ecosystems that place a premium on conformity and compliance, and unfortunately organizational design and practice, by and large, tend to be conformist. Organizations thus rarely recognize the enormous creative potential that lies within them. Secondly, it is commonly believed that creative ideation requires structured and systematic studies. Many managers and leaders who are steeped in scientific management cannot believe in the concept that ideas that are borne out of intuition, experience, or even that hypotheses can also be tenable and viable. Thirdly, those who control the intellectual reigns in organizations believe that effective ideation can be done only by personnel appropriately qualified and experienced, such as corporate planners, industrial engineers, or operational and business leaders, and so on.

If only the latent churn of ideas across the organizational pyramid could be harnessed, the power of mass ideation in organizations would be enormous. Assuming a typical employee joins a firm at the age of 25 years and retires at the age of 60, working 250 days a year, and 8 hours each day, he or she would have lived through 4,200,000 minutes of breathing and living through his or her firm. Given that a creative idea just needs a spontaneous spark, the typical employee would have at least several thousands of opportunities for ideation. Just a few of such ideation opportunities could become tools of excellence or triggers of game change. If only the organizational culture facilitates and encourages employees to be creative and expressive, and the organizational ecosystem captures and distils such creative ideas, creative ideation would receive significant institutionalization. In idea-centric organizations, such idea generation and capture occur from the very first contact between the employee and the company.

When I joined Telco (now Tata Motors) in 1974, nearly fifty years ago, as a Systems Analyst, almost the first question I faced in my induction program was whether I had any suggestions for the company! Senior leaders in Tata Motors consistently emphasized the power of ideas, motivating greenhorns as well as established managers to contribute with ideas. It is not surprising that the DNA of Tata Motors became one of sustained leadership in the development and manufacture of automobiles, indigenously. When Telco introduced its revolutionary semi-forward cowl (SFC) truck in the early 1970s, the creative instincts of every employee were channelled to make the development, manufacture, and post-introduction refinements an integrated institutional culture. Organizational culture plays a key role in stimulating and harnessing employee creativity.

Typically, there exist four phases in the life of an employee that give rise to different capabilities and opportunities for creativity. The first phase is the entry phase into the first job that provides the first opportunity to view the operations of the firm with a totally uncluttered perspective. To the extent that the employee is well equipped with academic tools, he or she can enhance the problem-solving capabilities of the organization. Clearly, it is the organization that must take the lead to harness the untested power of a new employee with an open, 'hear-her-out' approach. The second is the development and growth phase of the employee, say the next ten years of his or her career, wherein the employee understands the depth of the job, appreciates the nuances, and makes the work better. At the same time, this phase could be the most challenging, for the employees and their bosses, in terms of achieving the right conformity–creativity balance. The third phase could be the most opportunity-filled phase of an employee, with he or she, moving from an operating role to a managerial responsibility. It provides the twin opportunity of shaping strategy development as a manager heading a domain and mentoring his or her operating executive team members to tap their creativity. The fourth phase, say the last ten years of one's career, would be the game-changing phase where one, by virtue of being a cross-functional or business leader, would be vitally interested in unleashing and harnessing the power of organization-wide creative energy. Leaders of organizations could be the greatest advocates and beneficiaries of organizational creativity.

Black Boxes and White Spaces

Entity leaders need to appreciate that continuous and sustainable profitable growth is the essential facet of economic and social life. The judicious way a business leader manages the forces of competition, and the source of competitiveness determines the growth trajectory of the corporation. The business leaders have a unique responsibility in conceptualizing an integrated three-horizon platform of growth. The first horizon aims at excellence in the current business, the second horizon leverages the current business to exploit adjacent businesses, and the third horizon leads the corporation into uncharted but value building futuristic areas of growth. Employee creativity plays a notable role in each of the horizons, from continuous improvement in horizon 1 to step-function creativity in horizon 2 to breakthrough creativity in horizon 3. To harness employee creativity in this manner, the leaders should understand and respect the employee black box as a treasure-trove of ideas and seek out and pursue the environmental white space as a landscape of growth. Figure 3.2 presents the theory of cognitive neuroscience for supporting positive individual and organizational behaviour.

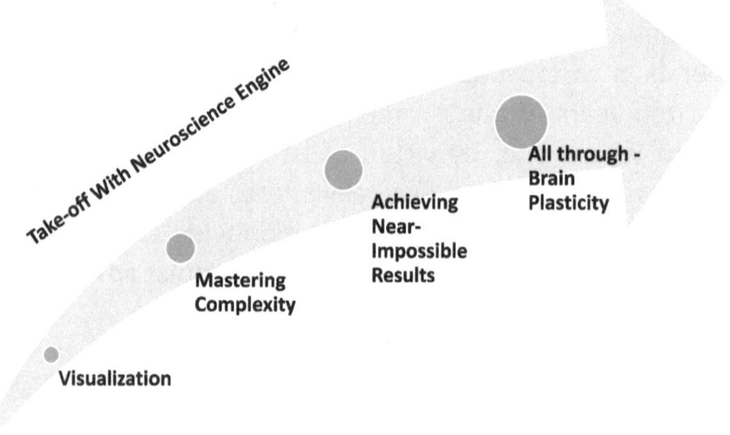

Figure 3.2: The Theory of Cognitive Neuroscience

Dr. V. S. Ramachandran, an eminent neuroscientist in the University of California, San Diego, in his path-breaking book "The Tell-Tale Brain" proposes strikingly that the human brain, with its 100 billion nerve cells and pathways, can make more connections than there are particles in the universe. The human brain is capable of being much more than a set of compartments for specific functions or even a complex set of electromechanical neuron network firing away based on internal and external stimuli. Cognitive neuroscience enables us to understand how a human brain could feel and appreciate its own deep consciousness. This sunrise science is an essential tool for employees and leaders of an organization to understand the power of the human brain that is otherwise sought to be severely limited by the way our organizations are designed for rigidity (often creating hard silos), the manner in which organizational processes are operated for conformity (which is often dictatorial), and the strategy by which development paths are rendered bumpy (laced as they are with ego–packed polemical speed-breakers).

The new science is anchored on the premise that every human brain that works in the organization is capable of visualizing previously unimagined latent growth vistas, mastering immensely complex skills, and performing seemingly impossible feats of development. Organizations whose employees and leaders appreciate the human brain as a dynamic force of creativity and not as an obscure black box of conformity would stand to gain immensely. The bar to achieving profitable growth is continuing to rise. It is passé today to seek excellence in the current business or attempt to gain business in contiguous spaces. Limits to efficiency in ongoing businesses are adversely set by the way day-to-day management is run in a complicated manner. At the same time, the entrepreneurial instincts, which are the very vitals of industrialization, are ebbed out by theories of strategic synergy and core competencies. Yet, whoever objectively surveys the deep history as well as the contemporary progress of industrialization understands that white space growth is the one that has the maximum potential of game-changing growth.

Very often, even large organizations with tremendous resources become wary of investing for white space growth, abjectly failing to do what a lone entrepreneur or a wise technocrat sets out to do despite resource crunch. Organizations should develop a healthy respect for the human brains in the organization (that are all waiting to express without their own conscious knowledge) and supplement it with a yearning for white spaces in the environment (that are all awaiting to be seeded with businesses that were never-before thought of). The way to benefit from the new neuroscience of organizational behaviour and the new paradigm of dynamic corporate strategy is to continuously drill for creative fuel in the organizational landscape and use the creative energy to build a pipeline of ideas that would drive growth. Organizations, like humans, must aim at and experience self-awareness to reach the full creative potential. Humans, in turn, must have the conviction and resilience to let their creativity prevail over the comfort of conformity.

Chapter 4

Humble Mastery

Robin Sharma is a passionate and committed speaker who shares several of his high-level thoughts on a pro bono basis. Amongst various teachers of management and coaches of leadership, there is probably no one else who renders his advice freely in both transactional and monetary senses of the term. He also rather walks the talk. It is not uncommon for him to make and release videos of his teachings even when he is on tours. Once, in a multicounty tour, for example, he released a video (The Princess + The Bentley) on how to achieve success and remain successful through certain precepts. While one may say that all of these constitute a carefully crafted global brand-building exercise, one cannot deny that they do contain nuggets of wisdom that appeal to, and influence, persons with an open mind.

Interestingly, Robin Sharma seems to believe that activities that do not add value in terms of personal and professional success need not, and should not, be performed. For him, intellectualizing one's mind is more value adding than entertaining it. He, therefore, comments in the video that rich people have large televisions, whereas successful people have large libraries. It is, of course, a moot point if success and richness are not correlated with each other! He even goes to the extent of rebuking Angry Birds game watching although viewed from another angle Angry Birds is a stupendous example of how creativity can result in great success in today's Internet-driven world. Be that as it may, three of his teachings in his video resonate well with certain important themes of this book. Figure 4.1 captures the three themes of Robin Sharma as a three-factor model of time-based learning mastery.

Figure 4.1: A 3-Factor Model of Time-based Learning Mastery

Using Time

Robin Sharma emphasizes that every moment of time is precious. According to him, a person realizes the value of time when he or she has a purpose in life. Without purpose, one may seem to be doing many things but often they could all constitute nothing but a meandering way of life. History was made by Telugu (an Indian regional language) director S. S. Rajamouli when he completed the magnificent and expensive movie epic in two parts "Baahubali–The Beginning" and "Baahubali–The Conclusion" and released the movies in 2016 and 2017, respectively, in over 4,000 screens globally to rave reviews and blockbuster collections. He went up a notch higher with another blockbuster "RRR" which received rare rave reviews from Hollywood celebrities and became an Oscar winner for its music. Anyone who tracks his directorial life can see the purpose in his life of being differentiated and distinctive in terms of each of his directorial ventures to date. Importantly, each has been more unique than the previous one.

Again, another history was made in Indian sports when Sania Mirza won the Wimbledon Women's Doubles title. Her life too has been one of purpose, from the time she displayed her tennis prowess in regional tournaments. Of late, many sportspersons from India have been winning global awards, with purposeful preparatory efforts. Time is a great enabler and calibrator of continuous improvement. A purpose as great as scaling the Mount Everest cannot be accomplished in a day; rather it requires continuous efforts and improvements, day after day. Each morning and each evening, we need to appreciate what we set out to achieve and what we have achieved, respectively. A mighty production like Baahubali or RRR may take five years to make but the whole process has an embedded higher purpose and ceaseless mastery. Time is a silent enabler and relentless critique of our purposefulness in life. There can be no better mirrors for transformation than a calendar and a clock, holding performance accountable to time!

Lasting Learning

Robin Sharma says, very rightly so, that one can never finish with learning in one's life. This is what Indian scriptures teach us too. Continuous learning and unceasing practice lead to mastery that has no limits. The neurosynaptic chips and the nano chips demonstrate how new nanotechnologies have provided tremendous computing power to systems based on these chips. For the first time, a true superconductor is likely to be unveiled with the invention of LK-99. Truly, there exist no limits or boundaries to knowledge. While certain fundamental laws could be immutable and timeless, experimentation and development would result in new continuous learning streams. Conversational AI and Generative AI are the new frontiers in intellectual pursuit. Continuous learning and development leads to all-round benefits, even as its ushers in new methods of doing things and makes a few established ways redundant, if not obsolete.

As the Japanese society demonstrates, taking personal and round-the-clock care of impaired elderly people is necessary, but the task can now be performed well by humanoid robots, watchful sensors, and remote management, all programmed for the purpose. Learnings may not always be new. In fact, several lifetime lessons may simply be embedded in oneself without immediate deployment. One must be thoughtful and mindful as well as introspective and reflective to rediscover, revisit, and redeploy them as new occasions demand. Learnings become virtuous when they are reinforced by neural triggering processes. For example, this chapter itself is triggered by Robin Sharma's video, triggering a combination of his teachings with the author's own beliefs. The ability to keep mind free, as Mahatma Gandhi and Rabindranath Tagore held, is an important facet of continuous learning that lasts a lifetime. It is left to everyone as to how open one would keep one's mind free to be able to absorb learnings continuously even as one is required to being decisive.

Humble Mastery

Mastery brings a rare capability and recognition to masters as they are recognized to be distinctly superior in their field or craft. Yet, masters who are humble have consistently won better acceptance than masters who are egoistic or arrogant. Arrogance spells failure to masters. The concept of humble mastery is important as mastery brings name and fame that, in turn, could lead to certain egoistic states in masters. Here, the awareness that as with learning there is really no end to mastery could make masters feel humble. Also, masters being in the company of other masters or in the practice of coaching bright disciples who could be shining new angles on existing knowledge could help masters stay humble.

Mastery over the domain must be accompanied by mastery over oneself for ultimate humility. The capability of "Sthita Prajna", as defined by Lord Krishna in the ancient Hindu epic Bhagavad Gita, connotes a stable wisdom that is primed by an ability to control oneself by inner thoughts and be unmoved by either attraction or repulsion as well as by happiness or remorse. Sthita Prajna is the ultimate state of self-control. While mastery in a domain could be a purpose, mastery over one's own self is also an essential purpose of life. Humility as a trait is a good shadow to have for one's personality even as it evolves over several learnings of life. Figure 4.2 presents a model of Sthita Prajna.

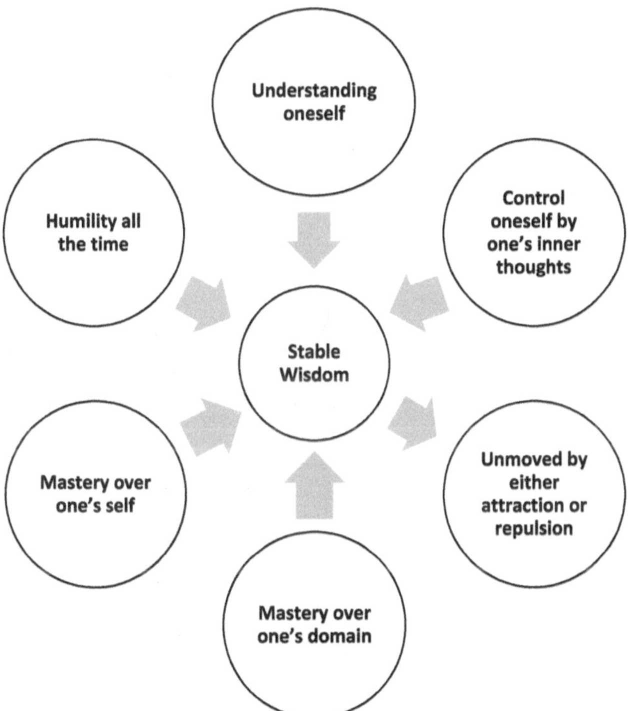

Figure 4.2: A Model of "Sthita Prajna"

More Sharing

I share several of my perspectives through my books and other publications. All such shared materials need not necessarily be found relevant by all, and for all situations. Nevertheless, I believe that the more one shares intellectually, the more the society benefits collaboratively. There would be anecdotal hyperboles occasionally like the sales manager of Bentley cars flying to the Volkswagen factory to get a paint that is an exact replica of the world's only one unique nail polish possessed by the princess. As with all anecdotes, the underlying moral is more important than the visible message! So is it with all passionate and positive sharing of perspectives in my books and publications. For me, the mastery of book-writing may seem to have been achieved when every sentence of the book is a nugget of wisdom. However, I realize that true mastery of my book-writing occurs when each of that nugget is persuasive and influential enough to make the reader a better person.

Chapter 5

Development through Role Models

Life is full of challenges and opportunities, and hence also full of fulfilments and disappointments. Life has several templates to grow or atrophy, materialistically and philosophically, as one moves through various stages of life, from birth to death. All wise parents try to set up a life that is full of opportunities and fulfilments for their wards. Unfortunately, due to factors beyond one's control, idyllic scenarios do not mostly happen, except for those borne with a silver spoon. As one gains the ability to independently analyse the life's challenges and opportunities, emulation–execution emerges as a conundrum that most individuals flirt with, and often, fail to get right. This chapter discusses a paradigm of emulation to achieve a superior state.

Emulation is the thought or act of trying to do something like someone whom one likes or admires does. Emulation is an attempt to try. Execution is carrying out of an action or activity in a manner that conforms to, or exceeds, the expectations set by, or perceived of, the role model. Emulation and execution are governed by an invisible but intrinsic factor called emotion. Emotion is the strong personal feeling that drives one towards both emulation and execution. The process of emulation is a life-journey process that is invisible and unrecognized for most time but is real and perpetual. Emulation, in formative years, occurs through family upbringing and pedagogy. Emulation in later years occurs through experiences and aspirations.

In the earlier formative stage, one is told explicitly to emulate a model behaviour, be it from the family, religion, history, or contemporary public life. In the later stage, one gets inspired or motivated by oneself to emulate a certain model behaviour. In the formative stage, execution is compelled by the system, be it the family or the institution, while in the later stage, execution flows from one's own belief that execution gets results. Obviously, there exist no cut-and-dried boundaries, as all through one's life the processes of emulation and execution keep taking place, most times with guidance (and sometimes with misguidance!), providing fulfilments and opportunities in this journey. If there could be a way to align opportunities, emulation, execution, and fulfilment in one's life, it would indeed be a great pathway to "materialistic nirvana!". Figure 5.1 summarises emulation, emotion, and execution.

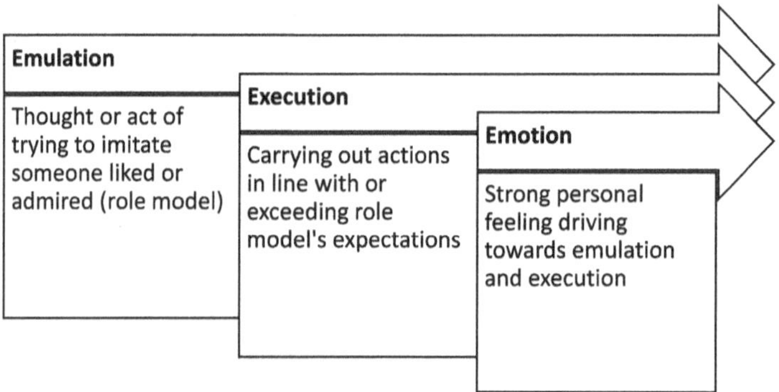

Figure 5.1: Emulation, Emotion and Execution

Worthiness, Practicality

Emulation is a part and pathway of life, and its existence cannot be denied. Emulation can occur in multiple ways, from a feature to a person, from a trait to a personality, and from an objective to a mission. There are, however, five common cautionary characteristics of emulation that an individual needs to be aware of. The first relates to the inability to judge for oneself whether one is emulating (or should be emulating) a person or what he or she stands for. For example, it would be one thing to believe that one should emulate Dr. Abdul Kalam (the reputed Scientist-President of India) and an entirely different thing to believe that one should emulate Dr. Kalam's erudition, simplicity, ethics, and passion. The second pitfall is the belief that emulation is around one role model. Here again, one tends to emulate, rather unknowingly, several people or several features for several reasons, and the ability to align or integrate multiple emulative processes is vital for comprehensive development. The third is a lack of understanding that emulation is an iterative process. While emulation cannot be opportunistic, it cannot also be ossifying; it is a continuous learning experience. The fourth is that emulation, oftentimes, has an emotive trigger; decluttering the emotional aspects is necessary for meaningful emulation.

The fifth caution relates to a perception that one needs to be independent, and never emulative; this, of course, is a fallacy and pitfall because even pioneers emulate another pioneering behaviour or mindset! In totality, the inability to introspect into one's own emulative behaviour often lands one in difficulties; more positively, understanding these aspects helps one achieve fulfilment from emulation. To be successful in emulation, one must consider two primary aspects of emulation: worthiness and practicality. First, whatever or whoever one emulates must fundamentally be worthy of emulation; the role model must be positive and capable of providing fulfilment or actualization. Second, it must be practical to emulate and execute. While heroic sagas have been written of amazing achievements even under the most challenging circumstances, they have been made possible because of certain accentuating features of the emulators. In other words, knowing what to emulate and how to emulate holds the key to successful emulation and fulfilment. It always pays to emulate a feature, trait, or an objective than a person, personality, or mission. Given that unknowingly, a person has multiple emulative triggers, it would be necessary to stay narrowly focused rather than broadly generic in emulation.

Competency, Completion

While worthiness and practicality are the essential parameters of emulation, emulation itself cannot be successful without execution. Execution has two facets: competence and completion. The desire to emulate must be backed by a passion to execute. Individuals who embark on risky programs of sportsmanship or creative arts leave conventional means of livelihood. Such people finally become successful as they get to understand and grow their competence well and remain relentless in their passion till they succeed in their task. The first step to successfully execute is, therefore, to understand the competency needed to execute. The second step to successfully execute is to understand the final step that defines the completion.

Individuals, unlike organizations, cannot outsource their competencies. Those who execute based on others' competencies eventually fail in non-native circumstances. Again, individuals, unlike organizations, cannot redefine completion. Unsuccessful organizations may be taken over and eventually prosper with accrued synergy, but unsuccessful individuals lapse into oblivion, relative to potential. At an individual level, therefore, every thought or act of emulation must be accompanied by an understanding of competency and completion. In this process, there is no better way than to emulate what the role model stands (stood) for, and how he stands (stood) for such a cause, effort, or result.

Biographies of great leaders or their own teachings constitute a great way to understand the "what and how" of emulation. Working with legends and role models in real time is an even greater opportunity. Being part of a great philosophical organization may lead to opening of one's mind on what one should look for. The irony of the situation is that many times individuals begin building competencies (like becoming a certified professional) and assuming an automatic outcome (like landing a good job) without understanding the larger purpose of emulation. Whether one's domain happens to be a matter of choice or circumstance, it is important for one to appreciate those aspects that are worthy of emulation and grasp what it takes to successfully emulate.

Transient versus Committed

As mentioned earlier, emotion plays a major role in the process of emulation; often, emotion is the first trigger for emulative thought. As one watches an exciting sport, one may feel that the sportsmanship displayed is worthy of emulation ("I wish I could play like Sachin!"). As one listens to a music program, one may feel that the musical talent evokes emulation ("I wish I could sing like SPB!"). As one gets swayed by a corporate leader, one may feel that the role model is all there to emulate ("I wish I could present like Steve Jobs!"). The point to note is that these tend to be transient thoughts of emulation, spurred on by emotional feel-good experiences and aspirations. Committed emulation, on the other hand, is a rational and diligent long-term process; even when spurred by emotion, it delayers emotion from logic to develop a sustainable basis for emulation.

Committed emulation connects an individual to what the leaders stand for as much as for the leaders themselves. Mahatma Gandhi's success was in connecting Indians to the values of Swaraj and Ahimsa and making them emulate those values for the larger national good. Committed emulation has both material and philosophical aspects to it. It recognizes the importance of being (or becoming) someone well recognized in the professional or social system on the strengths of one's capabilities. It must be, therefore, a matter of considered choice, even if it is triggered by emotion. One may, after a successful career stint, be emotionally attracted to be a social servant. It is important to logically analyse whether that worthy goal of emulation fits into oneself (or leads one to "what one is capable of becoming") by passing the idea through the four filters of worthiness, practicality, competency, and completion. Of the several emotive options that one encounters in each phase of life, these four filters would help one crystallize one's emulative thoughts effectively. An emulative process must mandatorily satisfy all the four criteria; drawing a blank on any of the four would lead to imperfect, if not negative, results.

Emulation as "Sadhana"

Sadhana is a Sanskrit word that means a quest to accomplish. Emulation is like sadhana. The goal must be carefully chosen, and the "sadhaka" (the one who is set on the path of sadhana) cannot, and will not, rest until the process of emulation is complete. Fortunately, in the classical systems of education, the concept of emulation as sadhana is ingrained. Most accomplished musicians gain their musical strengths through individualized apprenticeship under reputed musical legends.

The concept of house surgeon in medical education is aimed at letting young doctors learn the skill of medical practice from experienced physicians or surgeons. Even in a corporate setting, the practice of youngsters working as executive assistants with leaders is a way of apprenticing the youngsters in the art and science of management and leadership. As the number of talent seekers keeps expanding at the base, and as career development keeps becoming a more fast-paced race in the contemporary world, unfortunately, the apprentices as well as the leaders seem to be missing on the fulfilment of emulation.

In addition, those who still appreciate the need for emulation must realize that sadhana or emulation is a great anti-gravity effort. Non-emulative talent, like water, flows as per gravity to opportunities available. Emulative talent, on the other hand, scales new peaks with each phase of sadhana, based on committed and diligent efforts. Literally and figuratively, enlightened emulation is akin to intrepid mountaineering. The aim of emulation is not to create intellectual clones but to enhance the intellectual strength of the talent base in the country and the society. Typically, every society or every organization produces only a few natural leaders or maestros. As more people, whether of a society or an organization, seek to emulate the leaders and maestros for what they have accomplished and the virtuous paths thereto, the greater would be the combined intellectual strength of that society or organization. Figure 5.2 illustrates a model of sadhana in terms of a few avocations. The Figure presents how a normal learning position as a learner in select professions can be elevated to the level of sadhana, which requires greater application of thought and effort.

Goal as a Professional Expert	Learning Position as a Learner	Ideal Sadhana for the Learner
Doctor	House-Surgeon	Rotate in all fields of medicine and surgery
Executive	Intern	Learn all aspects of the avocation
Leader	Executive Assistant	Assist the leader and learn the ropes
Research Guide	Researcher	Drill down the existing theory and develop new theorem
Professor	Teaching Assistant	Assist, absorb and master the subject
Pilot	Co-pilot	Learn and earn the command
Maestro	Player	Follow the notes but learn the tunes
Master	Beginner	Evaluate and become a natural master

Figure 5.2: A Model of 'Sadhana' – Regaining the Missed Spirit

Chapter 6

Self-actualization as a Journey

Self-actualization must be the goal of every person, in a virtuous world. Self-actualization is the fact of using one's skills and abilities and achieving as much as one can possibly achieve. The concept of self-actualization is applicable for every individual of the society. The concept is not just employee centric. It is relevant for students aspiring to choose their careers and to entrants in organizations seeking to develop their careers. The unfortunate part, however, is that in the established system, most individuals would not be exposed to the concept of self-actualization, let alone enabled to explore it. As the concept is defined, there are two operative parts; one is that of skills and abilities, and the other is that of goals and achievements. Despite the simplicity and clarity of the concept, it is distressing that it is known and practised so little. A transactional approach of self-actualization is illustrated in Figure 6.1.

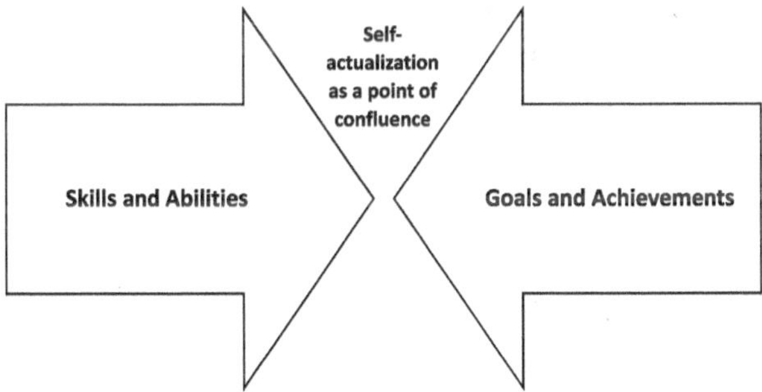

Figure 6.1: Self-actualization: A Transactional Approach

The primary reason is that the life of an individual from school to college during the education phase, and from the starting organization to the ending organization during the employment phase is seen in parts. A student's objective is no greater than selecting a helpful course; as a graduate the goal is no daunting than entering a remunerative job; and as a working professional, the aspiration is no loftier than reaching the top of a function, business, or company. None of these, however, leads one in a structured way to self-actualization. On the other hand, individuals tend to be ignorant of what they intrinsically seek to become – unfortunately, this remains the case even towards the terminal phase of their long careers. The reason is that individuals tend to compare themselves with others all the while than engage themselves in a process of self-discovery, and self-progress. It is important that one has a paradigm from the start of an academic journey to eventually self-actualize oneself.

Five Components

The journey of self-actualization is a five-component process. It starts with the discovery of one's skills and abilities as the fundamental building block. This is followed by converting the intrinsic capabilities into tangible competencies, in the process also acquiring synergistic capabilities. The third component is setting one's aspirations in a lens that is consistent with one's value systems and inner aspirations. The fourth component is leveraging one's competencies to achieve one's aspirations. This, in certain select cases of transformative leaders, involves converting individual self-actualization into an organizational, social, national, or global endeavour. India's freedom movement led by the Father of the Nation; Mohandas Karamchand Gandhi is a striking example of individual self-actualization helping a nation to actualize itself. The fifth level of self-actualization is an iterative one, assessing the level of self-actualization periodically, and going through the journey from a new phase of self-discovery each cycle. This could occur every few years, typically.

The fundamental starting point of self-actualization is self-discovery. The fundamental enabler of converting the intrinsic capabilities into tangible competencies is application. The fundamental motivator for aspirations is a larger purpose of life. The fundamental vehicle for converting aspirations into achievements is performance while the fundamental driver for transforming the individual self-actualization journey into a broader social transformation is authentic leadership. The fundamental driver for going through the iterative process is openness to understand the self in the context of contemporary and futuristic developments. Each of the components requires a high degree of clarity on the part of the individual. Self-actualization as a journey is neither easy nor one of mere followership. It is a journey of innovation and courage, a journey in which an individual grows with his or her broader residential unit, be it a classroom, a corporation, a society, a nation, or even the globe. Some of the greatest achievers actualized themselves in their laboratories or corporations but could simultaneously transform social and industrial living. Figure 6.2 presents the five enablers of self-actualization.

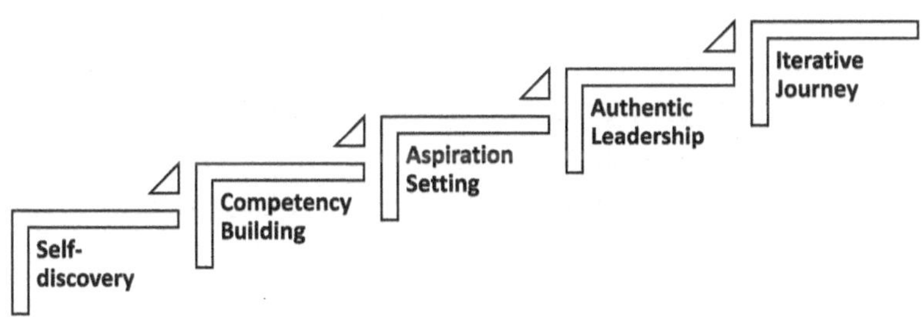

Figure 6.2: Five Enablers of Self-actualization

1. Self-Discovery

The fundamental building block of self-actualization is an awareness of one's intrinsic capabilities. Each human being tends to be blessed with certain capabilities genetically. This is true of even special individuals. These capabilities are accentuated or attenuated based on education, experience, and familial circumstances. However, the internal blinkers one has, often caused by family, educational, or career circumstances, inhibit one from understanding the full set of one's capabilities. The driver of a car may consider himself fit only for driving a vehicle all through his life but if engaged in the process of self-discovery, he may understand that his finely-honed skills of motor coordination could position him better for avocations requiring such skills, including music. A professional leader who charms her huge teams with her oration and charisma could well be capable of leading social and political movements. An academic who is passionate about strategy and entrepreneurship could one day become an industrialist himself or herself.

The paradox of being deployed by choice or default in one domain and having skills of another domain runs through one's life from educational to experiential states. The more visible of such trends is one of engineers starting with certain specializations but moving to other ones of aptitude or even business management. The subtler of such trends is one of pharmacists undertaking engineering of pharmaceutical plants and chemical engineers becoming chemists, as two examples. A process of open self-discovery is one of introspective understanding whereby one's skills, abilities, and aptitudes are appraised to help one discover one's path of self-actualization. Many times, friends, peers, and mentors play a helpful role in one's discovery process. Many times, organizational inequities, professional alienation, and social scorn, when tackled with a positive mindset could lead to self-discovery. The treatment meted out to M. K. Gandhi in South Africa challenged him to not only discover his capabilities but also recharter his life journey. The process of self-discovery constitutes, many times, an inflection point in one's life. It would launch one onto a journey of self-actualization, which would otherwise fail to be even recognized as possible.

2. Competency Building

It is not just sufficient for one to discover one's abilities, skills, and aptitudes. It is important to have the confidence and diligence to convert them into tangible competencies. The process of conversion is influenced by contextual setting as well as personal commitment. Contextual setting refers to the openness of the family, academic, or professional ecosystem that enables one to consolidate one's skills into competencies. When I was spotted as a writer of management columns in business papers decades ago while at Ashok Leyland, the managing director of the organization recognized my talent and gave me several opportunities to leverage my writing skills. The passion for writing and the opportunities it provided reinforced the communication skill as a core competence of mine. Personal commitment refers to the commitment of the individual to developing and deploying one's skills into, and as, competencies that the world recognizes. This is not a task that is easy by any reckoning if one is in a domain while one's skills are better related to another domain. Consider, for example, a person undergoing engineering education but has capabilities in as varied disciplines such as psychology and biology. It requires personal commitment to identify the domains through which he or she could leverage the intrinsic capabilities; in this case he or she may try to become a HR professional in an engineering company or become a biomedical engineer by postgraduate specialization.

Conversion of intrinsic skills into tangible competencies must be supported by a process of acquiring adjacent or adjuvant skills too. For example, a professional knowledge worker in an organization with a passion for social service would need to acquire communication skills to be able to actualize himself or herself. An engineer in the shop floor with a flair for industrial design would need to have the skills of understanding the marketplace to develop a canvas of actualization. The process of self-discovery would need one to identify the capabilities that are required to integrate one's intrinsic skills, convertible skills, and synergistic skills to develop a complete set of competencies. This requires a dedicated effort to learn the missing skills. Focused expansion of knowledge rather than random acquisition of degrees and certificates would be required. In one's competency-building exercise, the previous step of self-discovery, supplemented by benchmarking, helps one become a well-rounded personality of requisite competencies.

3. Aspiration Setting

The third component of the self-actualization journey pertains to aspiration setting. The aspiration can be set in a purely material sense (say, becoming the president or chief executive of a corporation), in a collaborative sense (say, developing the organization to a leading state), or in a highly emotional sense (say, becoming the change and transformation agent for the mankind). The aspirations could be also ranging between achieving something solely for oneself, for the family, or for the society. Between the extremes and around the middle exist many ways of looking for appropriate expression of aspirations. Let us imagine a professional leader who has all the attributes of becoming a chief executive but dislikes the materialism that surrounds the aspiration. Assuming he is in infrastructure industry, he could instead view his chief executive position as an instrument to build the nation with high-quality infrastructure and not necessarily as a chief executive position to aggrandize himself.

Similarly, a highly accomplished doctor or surgeon may look at building a hospital not merely to build business but also to serve the family and the community that brought him up. He may see himself as a saviour of more lives and a more effective provider of healthcare to a larger spectrum of population than he would individually be able to. In other words, in every material aspiration of rising to the pinnacle of an organization, there would also be a higher emotional aspiration of serving a larger community. Per contra, a sublime emotional aspiration would also need material power and an organizational vehicle to provide the harness to power the fulfilment of the aspiration. Competent professionals who baulk at the thought of material visibility as leaders would do well to appreciate that even the greatest of philosophers and religious leaders needed organizations and visibility to propagate their thoughts. All material aspirations have undertones of social service when power is exercised wisely, and all social aspirations need material backbone to be able to serve the society effectively. A self-effacing approach is not an option for an individual in the face of existence of competencies in him to serve.

4. Authentic Leadership

Given the competencies and aspirations, what remains as the last lap of the self-actualization journey is delivery. The bridge between competencies and aspirations is leadership. At the start of the academic career or professional career, leadership is a combination of the grassroots leadership of the individual and that of his or her leader. As one moves up the leadership hierarchy, individual leadership becomes more important and domineering while that of his leader becomes less domineering. Once one reaches the position of chief executive, he would have none other than the board to mentor. One must display leadership that is borne out of conviction about competencies and aspirations. The word "authentic," which means real, genuine, true, and accurate has great relevance to the actualization journey. The more authentic one is, the more leadership capabilities one gets imbued with. "Walking the talk" and "leading from the front" are two of the popular leadership adages that reflect the authenticity dimension in leadership journey.

Competencies, aspirations, and conviction form a successful triage of authentic leadership. An authentic leader is largely self-made. History teaches us that most top leaders of the world responded to circumstances and in several cases drew upon their inner sinews to fight adverse circumstances and shape positive circumstances. From Srinivasa Ramanujan, the greatest mathematician that India has produced to Mohandas Gandhi, India's apostle of nonviolence, authentic leadership was demonstrated through continuous performance leadership as opposed to armchair strategizing. Such leaders demonstrate that regardless of the domain, authentic leadership helps individuals actualize themselves, and in the process also help domain teams, societies, and nations achieve actualization. The transformation of individuals into professional leaders and change agents occurs through authentic leadership. A striking example is Dr. Pratap Reddy, the physician who returned from the USA to practice in Chennai, set up India's first corporate hospital, Apollo Hospitals, and later went on to transform Apollo Hospitals into a national healthcare chain and a great corporate brand, actualizing himself in the process as the leading healthcare icon of India.

5. Iterative Journey

Self-actualization is an iterative journey, which is characterized by constant rediscovery, continuous build-up of new competencies, setting of new aspirations, and reinforced leadership. Each iterative cycle takes the journey of actualization to the next higher level. The inability to actualize in one go is natural and not to be disparaged about. Just as corporations have horizons of growth, individuals too have their phases of development. From a single hospital in Chennai to a national hospital chain and a national pharmacy chain, the journey of the Apollo Hospitals group reflects the rediscovery of the actualization process by Dr. Pratap Reddy, the founder. When M. G. Ramachandran, N. T. Rama Rao, and J. Jayalalithaa moved out of their peak acting careers to enter the political arena and achieve resounding successes, such bold moves signified the processes of self-actualization into newer territories and onto higher trajectories. Creative fields are, in fact, well known for affording ample opportunities for enhanced levels of self-actualization. As a corollary, if individuals pursue paths of creativity, opportunities will abound for actualization.

The ultimate result of self-actualization goes beyond an individual achieving his or her full potential. Given that actualization is enabled by authentic leadership, individuals achieving self-actualization serve as change agents and role models. An authentic leader inspires trust as he or she tends to be a performing leader leveraging his or her competencies. He or she is also seen as a guardian of values. Actualization and leadership do not necessarily mean that as the cliché goes one must always lay a new path. There cannot, for example, simply be as many ways of studying science, engineering, or management as there are students. Similarly, there cannot but be only a few ways of designing, manufacturing, and marketing products. What distinguishes one individual from the other in studies is studious absorption and creative application. What distinguishes one corporation from the other in execution is efficiency and effectiveness. From individual leadership in the initial years to corporate or organizational leadership towards the senior years, self-actualization tends to be a highly thoughtful, competency-based, aspiration-pursuing journey of authentic leadership.

Chapter 7

Career and Life Phasing

In today's world of increased longevity, the career span for a typical talented executive has significantly lengthened. As a result, the new generation could be expected to have a long career span of five decades, from 25 to 75 years of age. Compared to the current and older generations who coasted along the career paths (retiring at a 'ripe-young' age of 55 or 58 years!), the new generation has the aggression and aspiration to shape their careers in an accelerated manner (without resting till they reach the 'young-ripe' age of 70 or 75 years!). Retirement from active life in the current times happens more by individual preferences or health and wellbeing considerations rather than by mere employment or social norms.

Another new trend is shaped by the new generation's quest (and the parental pressures) for joining elite institutions and premium courses to leverage into companies and careers of potential high net-worth in future. This has led to a phenomenon of rapid and early career burnout in most other cases, denying to such people long-term opportunities of a career marathon. With a bit of philosophical reasoning, external awareness, and candid introspection, one would surmise that in life, the law of averages would eventually work out in most cases. There are, in fact, four laws that govern career life, understanding of which would provide an appropriate perspective to appreciating the long-term realities of career life. Once these realities are appreciated, it would be possible to look at a more orderly and structured progression of career life. Hinduism prescribes four stages of life for a typical male. Shakespeare has formulated seven stages of life in his play "As you like it." This chapter hypothesizes four stages of life for career aspirants so that the new generation can face the corporate life with equality and stability. First though, the four laws of organizational life need to be appreciated.

The Four Pyramidal Laws

The first law of organizations is the Law of Pyramids. Whatever the nomenclature and colour given to the structural dispensations of organizations, the enduring law is that any organization is a pyramid in terms of departments and people. In fact, the typical organization tends to be several pyramids within a master pyramid. Each time one reaches the apex of a pyramid (read: department), he or she will find that that place is, in fact, the bottom of another pyramid (within the overall pyramid). The second law of organizations is the Law of Slippery Walls. Like pyramids that offer no easy steps or holds to climb, organizational pyramids also offer no easy way to climb to the top. The path is steep and slippery, almost inevitably. The third organizational law is the Law of Multiple Climbers. This law teaches that even if one is fortuitous to be alone on the climb on one's side of the wall, there would inevitably be many climbers from the other sides of the pyramid (read: sections, departments, or businesses in place of walls, depending upon which level of pyramid one is trying to perch oneself onto!).

The fourth organizational law is the Law of the Spiked Chair. This law, which is the most profound of the four laws, can only be experienced and not taught. It states that if one succeeds in climbing up the pyramid with one's diligence and persistence, and fair amount of luck, one will find the apex far too sharp and spiked to afford any chance of comfortable stay. Unfortunately, there would be no honourable climb-down either. Whoever reaches the apex of the ultimate pyramid would, no doubt, wonder why at all he or she has aspired for, and worked towards, reaching the apex of the organizational pyramid. However, just as everyone despairs about life looking at others' travails (be it studies, jobs, or marriage) but goes through the same rigmarole, the members of organizations go through the motions of climbing pyramids multiple times with great zeal and application. Those who understand the four laws in a philosophical perspective would, however, be in a state of equanimity to understand and pass through structured career phasing. Figure 7.1 presents the four pyramidal laws.

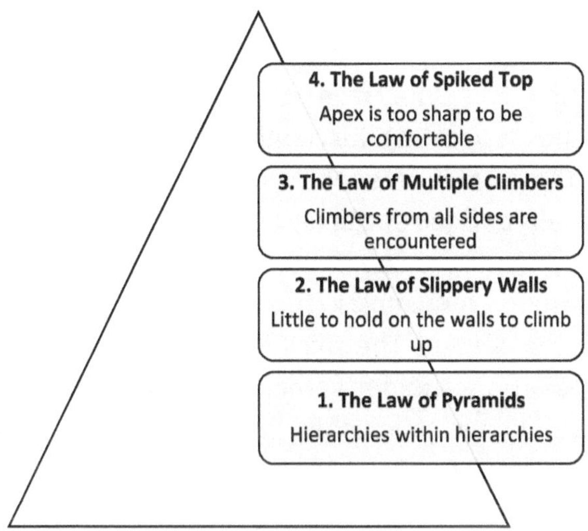

Figure 7.1: The Four Pyramidal Laws

Four Phases of Life

Hinduism classifies one's life in terms of four phases or stages, each being called ashrama. The first stage is the "brahmacharya" or the student stage. The second stage is the "grihastha" or the householder stage. The third stage is the "vanaprastha" or the hermit stage. The fourth and final stage is the "sanyasa" or the ascetic stage. Without going into the full details of what each stage is expected to involve in a classic Hindu way, it would be sufficient to understand the basic purposes of each of the four stages of life, which somewhat unfortunately are focused only on the male members. The student stage is a period of formal education. It lasts until the age of 25, during which period, the young person seeks to attain, under a famed guru, both spiritual and practical knowledge. During this period, he is prepared for his future profession, as well as for his family. This is a phase wherein the greatest dedication and application is expected of the young learner.

The second period of householder begins when a man gets married and undertakes the responsibility for earning a living and supporting his family. At this stage, Hinduism supports the pursuit of wealth as a necessity, and indulgence under certain defined social and cosmic norms. This ashrama lasts until around the age of 50. However, given the rigors of the subsequent two stages, the second stage virtually lasts a lifetime these days! The third stage of a man begins when his duty as a householder comes to an end: his children are grown up and have established lives of their own. At this age, he should renounce all pleasures, retire from his social and professional life, leave his home, and go to live in a forest hut, spending his time in prayers. This kind of life is indeed very harsh. No wonder this third ashrama is now nearly obsolete. In the fourth and final stage, a man is supposed to be totally devoted to God. He is a "sanyasi", and he has no home or no other attachment; he has renounced all desires, fears and hopes, as well as duties and responsibilities. He is virtually merged with God, and all his worldly ties are broken; his sole concern becomes attaining "moksha," or release from the circle of birth and death (suffice it to say, very few can go up to this stage of becoming a complete ascetic). The caveat here is the equity and equality demand the observance of a similar format to the female members of the society.

Figure 7.2 is a schematic of the four phases of career growth.

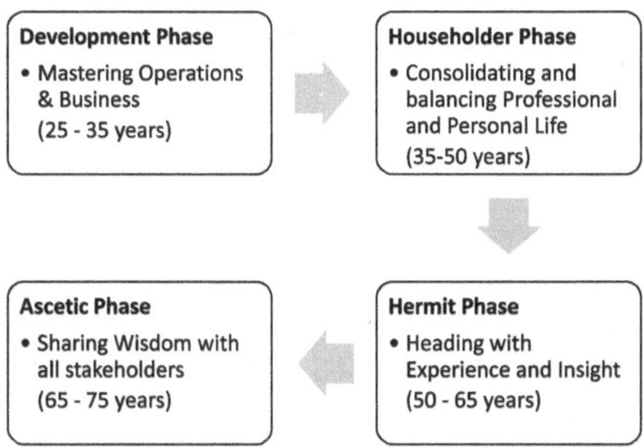

Figure 7.2: The Four Phases of Career Growth

Four Career Ashramas

Given that the career span of the talented new generation is tending to be five decades long, one may hypothesize four distinct phases, which have similar intentions and applications as in progression of life. In the first phase, or the first decade of the career (say, age 25 to 35 years) that may be called the development phase, the incumbent must, irrespective of prior education and background, be focused on learning. The first phase represents the golden phase to master the products, processes, domains, and businesses of a corporation. The more one learns and applies the knowledge as one learns, the stronger will be the foundations of one's career. The stronger the foundation, the bigger and taller can be the superstructure. It is also important to secure the right guru or mentor during the learning phase. The second phase, which corresponds to the householder phase, is the real career-building phase. This phase or the second decade and half of the career (say, 35 to 50 years) represents the period of bounty to generate wealth for the corporation, and simultaneously stabilize professional and personal life balance by providing security and prosperity to the family through his earnings. This is the phase when the aspirant needs to bring out all his energy and enthusiasm to lead and manage teams, climb up the slippery pyramids, and reach positions of substance. At the end of the phase, the career aspirant would have typically arrived.

The third phase, which corresponds to the hermit phase, is the stage when one brings one's experience and wisdom to become a leader, who is expected to lead from the top. This stage, corresponding to 50 to 65 years of age, is one where the incumbent starts becoming increasingly lonely, with both his competitor groups and partner groups becoming thinner. As a hermit discovers truth through prayers, the leader in this phase discovers the larger purpose of leading an organization, which is beyond professional growth or personal riches. The truth as one would understand in this phase is to satisfy multiple stakeholders and craft an executable vision. The fourth phase, which corresponds to the ascetic stage, is represented by the last 5 to 10 years of career life (say, 65 to 70 or 75 years of age). Clearly, this phase represents one of organizational nirvana for a leader. This is the phase wherein highly capable leaders become non-executive chairpersons of corporations or become advisors and mentors to for-profit and not-for-profit organizations. They start looking for leaders who would fulfil or improve upon their legacy. Those in the first phase of learning could ideally lock themselves to mentors of the fourth phase to establish the right "parampara" (line of successors).

Journey, not the Destination

As one grapples with the four pyramidal laws of career development and undertakes the rollercoaster ride through the four phases of life, reaching in the process the narrow and sharp apex, one understands that the journey of organizational life is more important than the destination itself. Some, if not all, would muse that the fortune of satisfied life tended to be more at the bottom of the pyramid rather than at the top. If only there would be a way for the young career aspirants to fast-track themselves through the organizational time machine to simulate and assimilate the philosophical learning, there would be an opportunity for them to savour the journey of corporate growth through contributions each day, rather than waiting to occupy the sharp peak to make an elusive impact. For most people, an incremental contribution each day, from the very first day of a five-decade career could be more rewarding than the aspiration of creating a stunning impact at the helm, decades later.

Chapter 8

Humility in Success

In human-human interactions, human-organization, and organization-organization interactions, we encounter all the time individuals and institutions displaying diverse traits, each at different points of a respective spectrum. For example, we may encounter individuals who are optimistic or pessimistic or at various points in an optimism–pessimism spectrum. Similar positioning could be true of institutions as well; some institutions would never abandon the growth path despite adversities and some immediately downsize at the first sign of demand recession. The number of such traits on which individuals and institutions can be so classified are many. However, two traits that govern the relationships within and between individuals as well as institutions are extremely critical to individual and institutional development.

The two traits that are particularly important in this context are humility and arrogance. These two traits are the visible or felt expressions of how individuals and institutions think or behave with and among each other. While these are commonplace words, they are also commonly misunderstood; it is, therefore, worthwhile to recall their essence. Humility is the endearing way of thinking and behaving that comes from considering that one is not necessarily better, smarter, or more important person than other people, whether one is or not. Arrogance, in direct contrast, is the insulting way of thinking and behaving that comes from believing that one is better, smarter, or more important than other people, whether one is or not. Like all positive and pristine traits, humility is hard to ingrain while, like all negative and crude traits, arrogance is easy to embrace. Figure 8.1 depicts a causative framework of individual and institutional humility and arrogance.

	Humility	**Arrogance**
Individual	• Unique trait related to genetics and upbringing. • Backed by knowledge, experience, wisdom, and self-worth.	• Modified trait acquired through environmental dynamics. • Boosted by premature and artificial or superficial success. • May be backed by knowledge and experience too
Institutional	• Unique trait related to policies on trusteeship and social responsibility. • Backed by successes in performance and growth.	• Modified trait acquired through accolades of industry leadership and traits of leaders. • May be backed by performance and growth too.

Figure 8.1: A Causative Framework of Individual and Institutional Humility and Arrogance

Fusion, Diffusion

Ironically, behaviour and action patterns that are so dissimilar as humility and arrogance are built on common foundations. Perceptions of knowledge, capability, competence, and accomplishment usually drive one's own as well as others' belief of what one is. It is human nature to continuously evaluate oneself and others on these aspects and position oneself to be superior or inferior vis-à-vis others. It is easy to feel egoistic (which is just a step away from arrogance) in the context of one's superiority and feel defeatist (which is just a step away from worthlessness) in awareness of one's inferiority. In contrast, it requires a special kind of personality disposition to be humble despite superiority and strong despite inferiority. This challenge is compounded as one receives continuous feedback, direct and indirect as well as genuine and timeserving, from one's network.

These traits are independent of differentials in competence of stratified groups of individuals. For example, a teacher is naturally required to be highly knowledgeable compared to the students. That does not bestow any right to be arrogant on the part of the teacher because that differential capability is the fundamental basis of such teacher–student relationship. On the other hand, a great teacher remains humble by believing that he or she needs to learn more to teach better, and even accepts the occasional brilliant repartees and queries from the students. Similarly, a manager or a specialist by virtue of his or her experience ought to know more than his or her staff but, by no means, it is an unnatural accomplishment that should make the manager or specialist even a wee bit arrogant. On the other hand, a great manager or specialist always looks to expand his or her frontiers of knowledge besides welcoming the fresh thoughts of youngsters and peers, all with humility.

Trending, Branding

Institutions have a different set of influencers. Their competence is reflected in terms of their market share and profitability. As a result of their achievements on these two dimensions, they trend as performers, and as performers they get branded too. Most start-ups and young firms achieve this by being capable as well as humble. However, with positive trending and branding, they keep acquiring scale. Most institutions as they grow in scale face an inflection point, unique in each case, from which level they start behaving and acting less vulnerable and more invincible. Akin to the propositions related to individuals earlier, this also represents a humility–arrogance tipping point. Scale of operations often leads to distance, between employees and the management, within employees, and more importantly between organizations and their customers.

At and from such an inflection point, an institution starts believing that it knows what is right—for itself as well as its employees and customers. The level of functional specialization and sophistication of data analytics may well sustain the arrogant institutions on the performance journey, but such arrogance will radically alter how they are perceived in terms of their relative humility and arrogance. For example, an increment letter that arrives in the mailbox of each employee of a one-lakh-employee-strong company as immediately as the day after the close of the performance year, despite its efficiency, would be perceived to be cold and impersonal (which is a step or two away from arrogance). If in that organization, the increment letter, duly signed by a CXO, is personally handed over by the manager to each employee (even if with a few days of delay), the act would reflect continuing institutional care (which is a shade or two closers to humility).

Interlays, Interplays

Adding complexity to the situation is that humility and arrogance are capable of being faked. An individual or institution may be intrinsically arrogant but may make it appear as aggression (which is considered a surrogate for competitiveness!). Others may cultivate humility as a facade and as a means to an end, notwithstanding not-so-modest views of themselves. Some individuals or institutions may take humility to the extremes of perpetual silence and acceptance, leading to doubts on intrinsic capability (also, as surrogates of passive aggression). Others may alternate between flashes of arrogance and glints of humility to reconcile their inner contradictions. Given that human nature is not perfect, having humility inside and faking aggression outside or vice versa is hardly an appropriate state of individual or institutional thought and action.

The ideal ecosystem would comprise interactions on three dimensions, between individuals, between individuals and institutions, and between institutions. In terms of levels of endowments or competencies, the players can never be equal, but the relationships can certainly be equitable. Individual-level collaboration, between the competent and not-so-competent, is the foundation of building humility in the organizational ecosystem. Collaboration between individuals and institutions, despite the institution being the all-powerful giver and the individual being the weaker receiver, constitutes the foundation of the social ecosystem. Collaboration across value chain constitutes the foundation of the industrial ecosystem. An original equipment manufacturer (OEM) could be endowed with better marketing and financial power than a small component maker but the former ought to be cognizant of the essentiality (and not the optionality) of the component maker to the OEM.

Gross, Subtle

When concepts such as humility and arrogance are discussed, the focus tends to be on the visibly gross or misleadingly subtle aspects of the concepts. Just as being silent is not being humble, being in an agreeing or obsequious mode does not constitute humility. Similarly, proposing or communicating an alternative way of thought or action does not reflect lack of humility (let alone display of arrogance). Humility is the ability to convey what is correct and appropriate to context and content in a manner that does not reflect superiority, and in a manner that the recipient is inspired to absorb the context. Humility is the ability to learn as much as possible and relevant from other individuals and institutions. In the ultimate analysis, humility is the ability to share, spread, and enhance as well as also absorb knowledge in a collaborative and inspirational manner.

In a similar manner, arrogance does not mean only the insulting way of thought, expression, or action. Arrogance can be very subtle too. When sales executives in a retail store of iconic brands chat amongst themselves for minutes without connecting with customers, it is nothing but institutional arrogance. When members of organizations, private or public, provide inadequate responses or take inordinate time to serve stakeholders, that too is institutional arrogance. In several cases, the line between individual and institutional arrogance is rather thin. Humility needs to be a key anchor of family and organizational culture to be able to nurture humility and eliminate arrogance in individual members.

Relational Matrix

While we have all grown to accept humility as a rare sparkle and arrogance as a common inevitability of high-stress life, we need to take a break and recognize the insidiously harmful effects of lack of humility or exertion of arrogance, gross or subtle, on enhancing stress levels in the society. We should aim to develop greater and more perceptive understanding of these commonly misunderstood concepts and reflect on them through a Humility–Arrogance Relational Matrix (HARM). Fundamentally, being humble, knowing one's limitations, is a source of strength but being humble with all the awareness of one's competences is an even greater source of strength. Similarly, forsaking ego in oneself, despite the weaknesses of others, is a source of strength but eschewing ego despite the awareness of one's superiority is an even greater source of strength.

Four combinations are possible. Individuals can be humble, but institutions can be arrogant, especially commercially and rapidly successful organizations; it requires individuals to persevere even as it behoves key decision-makers to launch a culture journey in institutions. Individuals can be arrogant but institutions, especially service-oriented and non-governmental organizations can be humble; it requires individuals to reflect and remediate even as the organizations persevere on their path. Both individuals and institutions can be arrogant; this could be a concomitant of a despotic culture that smothers creativity and demands servility; mercifully such combinations are few but unless they are transformed, the overall national ecosystem will be at risk. In the virtuous grid, the individual as well as the institution would be competent and capable; such individuals and institutions would certainly render a great service to the nation by being less modest about their uniqueness and imbibing other individuals and institutions with their implicit drivers of humility.

Success through Humility

On May 9, 2014, an interesting article appeared in the Times of India titled "Humility makes CEOs from India Stand Out," which hypothesized that the ascent of Indian origin leaders as CEOs in global corporations is related to Indians being humble by nature. The reference has been, among others, to Indra Nooyi, Chairperson of Pepsi, Satya Nadella, CEO of Microsoft, Nitin Nohria, Dean of Harvard, and Rajiv Suri, CEO of Nokia Networks. There is no doubt that persons from outside the

Western world would find it hard to reach apex positions in Western-headquartered global corporations. This is as unsurprising as a Western executive finding it difficult to be at the helm of a Japanese corporation. National culture probably has as much role as notional competence in influencing leadership choices. The ascent of Indians to CEO positions is, therefore, remarkable, and noteworthy.

The article quotes Govind Iyer, managing director of Egon Zehnder India, a leading executive search firm; Govind states that humility is the key to being a respected leader as that means the leader is receptive towards learning and professional growth. He also clarifies that humility does not mean that one cannot be aggressive and extrovert. He emphasizes that these qualities need to be displayed with humility. Rajiv Burman, managing director of Lighthouse Partners, another executive search firm hypothesizes in the article that given the strong emphasis in the Indian culture on family and social relationships, Indian leaders work very effectively in groups with humility. Vivek Chandra, country manager-India, Harvard Business Publishing considers that leaders who develop higher self-awareness tend to be humbler. In the same article, Lynda Gratton, professor of management practice is quoted as saying that emphasis on authenticity and inner journey is a characteristic of changing leadership expectations.

Hard and Soft

Leaders are expected to lead. It is therefore believed that leaders must exert their presence with knowledge, expression, and execution through which they must be able to influence and align their followers. Aggression and extroversion, enjoying success every bit openly, are also considered good additions to a successful leadership profile. These may well be the "hard" qualities that define leadership. Leadership built only on these hard factors tends to be vulnerable to performance dips even if performance drivers are beyond the leader's control. Leaders need certain "soft" qualities that help the leaders go beyond driving and influencing. Soft qualities are those that endear leaders to their followers. They help the leaders connect with their followers and even non-followers sustainably. Mahatma Gandhi is an enduring example of soft qualities adding sheen and sustainability to leadership. Humility has been the most prominent of Gandhi's soft leadership qualities.

The role of humility in influencing leadership development is not well understood. Humility is the quality of being humble. Humility is the quality of thinking that one is not better than others (although one's achievements or others' opinions may imply so). One's humility is never expressed but is invariably felt and experienced by others. Humility can never be a sign of weakness or passivity; rather it stems out of one's conviction and courage, in a sense. Winston Churchill stated that while it requires courage to stand up and speak out, it also requires courage to sit down and listen. This is an interesting concept. Individuals who are humble to face constructive challenges are often able to discover their own abilities or learn new capabilities that help manage them. The earlier-discussed aspect of self-awareness is the foundation for developing authenticity that is capped by humility.

Authentic Humility

Figure 8.2 is a model that presents the markers and drivers for authentic humility. Awareness that leads to knowledge and competencies, and self-awareness that leads to self-improvement are the ideal combination to make an individual or a leader hugely successful. The key to sustaining such success lies in humility; humility that teaches one that success need not be worn on one's sleeve, humility that teaches that failure is a result of lack of humility, humility that teaches that there can always be scope for self-improvement, humility that teaches one to respect others, and humility that enables the development of individuals or leaders to excel themselves. It is important to note that if power and presence are required in certain contexts, they are effectively provided by stature and humility as much as by knowledge and execution. Dr. Abdul Kalam, occupying the highest office of the President in India, was always an epitome of humility. He never lost his connect with children and demonstrated his humility spontaneously and naturally through his child-like interactions but with an enlightened objective of raising their social and intellectual awareness. The humility of Dr. Abdul Kalam was never lost on the huge nation.

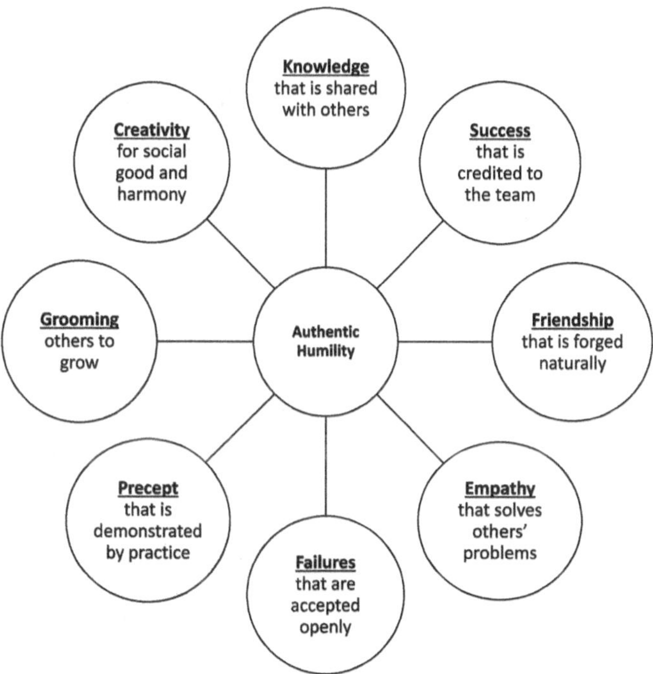

Figure 8.2: Markers and Drivers of Authentic Humility

Like most emotions or soft skills, humility also can be an affected behaviour and not a real and genuine behaviour. Individuals can put up a charade of humility. However, authentic humility is easily distinguished from affected humility. Self-awareness is the key to genuine humility. It enables people to overcome their shortcomings through greater and better awareness and appreciate others' superiority or need for support to others. A self-aware leader creates success by working with and leveraging the capabilities of other competent peers. Mahatma Gandhi's humility helped him reach out to the nation on one hand and work with other capable leaders on the other. At the institutional level as well, successful institutions that are humble are likely to achieve far greater and sustainable success than other institutions that are smug on success or impervious to criticism. If Toyota had to face unexpected recalls, it was due to a belief that the best was always being done and if Toyota still retained brand equity and went on to achieve global leadership in the automobile industry year after year, the reason lies in its humility to accept that even the best was not good enough, and there was scope for self-improvement.

Chapter 9

Mobile Body and Agile Mind

Human life is one of the greatest gifts of God. It is also one of the most complex phenomena in terms of predictability and management. The multiple destinations one reaches in one's life journey, and how fulfilling some of the sub-journeys would be, in many ways, are beyond one's control. For centuries, therefore, the Hindu religion, spirituality, and philosophy analysed the phenomenon of human life in terms of multiple models that balance materialism and spiritualism and harmonize existentialism and nirvana. All through the models and paradigms of life, the need to keep one's mind and body healthy comes through as a constant underlying thought. Over the centuries, human race has learnt to understand itself and the environment better and seek increasing comfort and security for itself. Modern lifestyle and modern medicine are products of such awareness. Yet, there remains much more to fathom. Worse still, the human race's solutions of industrialization and commercialization have created new problems, from profligacy and pollution to domination and exploitation.

Economic growth with social equity continues to be a distant goal even in the most advanced countries. The knowledgeable individual is at crossroads today. He or she must compete on the current rules of society to live a useful life. He or she also is painfully aware that relentless competition, without matching competency, is not a winning game either. The Indian family system has been providing a safety valve; the current generation invariably gives up competition at some point of time and expects its future generation to become what it has failed to become (or has given up becoming). Even the family safety valve is now getting clogged. Life seems so remorseless, for the young and old alike. Multiple options influence and beckon the young, and a crumbling joint family and community system stares at the elders. In a sense, and probably in the only logical sense, the individual in the contemporary world has no one except himself or herself to rely upon. The mushrooming of spiritual leaders and institutions points to the fact that the Indian individual, young or old, is yet to come to grips with the challenge of self-management and needs support and guidance. Yet, the prescription for a fulfilling life, independent of any stream of religion, spirituality, or philosophy could be just very simple: a mobile body and an agile mind!

Good Life, Balanced Life, or Wholesome Life?

Everyone seeks a good life; unfortunately, like the multiple meanings the word "good" has, the word "good life" has also different meanings for different people. Some of the meanings or implications of good are high quality, pleasant, sensible, favourable, morally right, skilful, rule abiding, kind, and thorough, to take some of the more prominent or popular meanings. Generally, good reflects agreeable. Good life does not differentiate between personal life and professional life, which can be described by all these nuances in varying degrees. A natural flaw in one's pursuit of good life is that as a goal it is highly individualistic and enables high variability unrelated to one's capabilities and environmental positioning. Of late, there is a view that individuals in the competitive world tend to maximize returns from their professional life to pursue a good personal life. This has led to two types of professionals. The first type is for whom work has become a passion, an obsession, and an end by itself, leading to individuals becoming workaholics who utterly neglect their personal side. Here personal does not mean merely family life but it also means the life space necessary for one's own development. This has led to the formulation of the concept of work–life balance. This concept of balanced life, again, is a highly variable concept that leaves the options to individuals to define the balance and the goodness within each life segment.

There is a third concept of wholesome life, which this chapter proposes, that could be an alternative to the apparently determinate concept of good life and the rather indeterminate concept of work–life balance. Wholesome life covers the physical and intellectual dimensions of life. It is a holistic concept of life that combines the concepts of goodness and balance in terms of what one can deliver for oneself and one's family as well as for one's organization, society, and nation. Every individual, from the mason who constructs a laboratory, to the scientist or the engineer who operates the laboratory and its equipment, and the financier who funds a project qualifies for the concept of wholesome life. The dimension of physical wellbeing is ignored while that of intellectual life is misunderstood. Neither of these can be pursued independent of the other and, in fact, the two dimensions are interrelated, interdependent, and even synergistic.

Physical wellbeing is often seen by this generation in terms of athlete-grade strength, lean frame, and even sleek abdominal muscles. There is no uniform prescription, however. It appears that Covid-19 in general and Long-Covid in particular have created unknown imbalances for the young and old alike. The real wellbeing must be customized; it is maintaining oneself strong, stable, and self-reliant with optimal physical alertness and responsiveness under normal circumstances and with assured resilience under conditions of stress or sickness. Physical wellbeing is part genetic, but it is largely developed through a lifetime as well. Intellect is often linked with formal education. Everyone has, and does exercise, one's intellect. The mason who judges the heights and slopes understands the strength and the malleability of steel, knows the right proportioning of concrete, and builds the building brick by brick with the right tolerances has as much intellect as a civil engineer would have in respect of construction. The physical and mental wellbeing are determined by two factors: mobile body and agile mind. Figure 9.1 summarizes the dilemmas of life, and the need for a hybrid outcome.

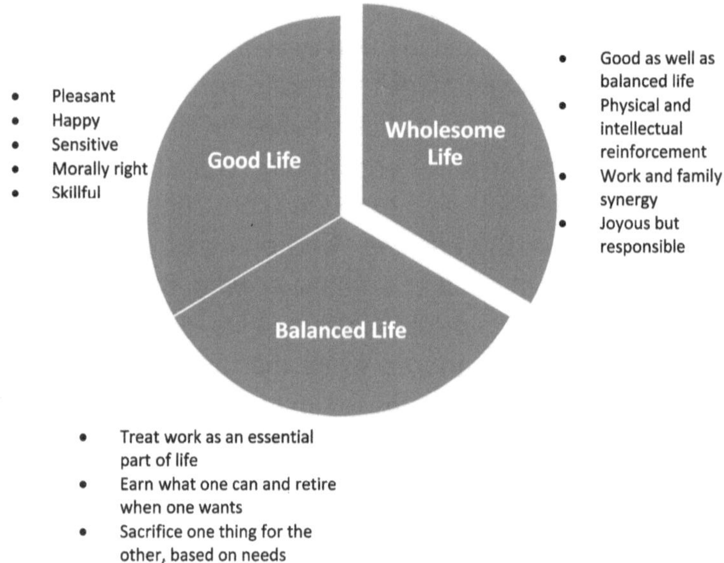

Figure 9.1: The Dilemmas of Life: Need for a Hybrid Outcome

Mobile Body

Human body is a wonderful musculoskeletal system that is operated by the brain through the neurological and blood capillary systems, among others. Not one of the human body systems is less or more important than the other. However, amongst all the human tasks, maintaining physical mobility or movement must rank amongst the highest priorities of life. Mobility is the essence of life; the more mobile a person is in terms of using all the limbs and muscles, the healthier and more productive he or she would be for himself or herself, his or her family, and the larger organizations and communities. Today's industrialization favours largely sedentary lives (office environments) or stationary lives (factory environments) with minimal human effort. It, therefore, devolves on the individuals to achieve as much mobility as possible, both at work and off work.

Safety and mobility are highly related. The more stable and safer a person is, the more mobile he or she is likely to be. Conversely, the more unstable and unsafe a person is, the more immobile the person is likely to be. Walking, running, jogging, sprinting, and climbing are some of the mobility options one can 'exercise'. Office systems that confine people to eye movements on computer screens, and factory systems that limit people movements to machine movements all the time are invitations to progressive immobility. If one understands the scientific kinetics of movements well, one can master the intricate dynamics of personal productivity. Every human discovery, made ostensibly to make life more secure and comfortable, has ended up creating new problems. To provide flexibility of indoor walking, motorized treadmill has been invented. It has brought in its wake problems of unnatural impact of walking and running for its users. To cater to the need to provide safety and comfort, running and jogging shoes have been created. They have started modifying the kinetics of using the foot.

The personal automobile has emerged as one of the greatest inventions, but it has ended up enhancing travel efficiency and curbing physiological mobility at the same time. Escalators and elevators, ideal for the aged and handicapped, are mobility-curbing temptations even for the young and fit. The march of technological progress is relentlessly oriented towards curbing body mobility. It is, therefore, necessary to make mobility an essential ingredient of one's daily life. It will boil down to how one makes time for mobility. Five factors determine safe mobility for a human being in his or her quest for quick mobility. Safe mobility can be achieved by choosing the appropriate base of support for the feet, low centre of gravity, appropriate positioning of the centre of gravity over the base of support, movements aligned to body mass and weight, and the coefficient of friction of the movement surfaces. There is more physics and engineering to the science of safe physiological mobility than is commonly recognized. Daily exercise routines and office/factory ergonomics must integrate the kinetics of safe mobility in day-to-day life.

Agile Brain

On the face of it, if physical mobility is the essence of physical wellbeing, mental agility is the essence of mental wellbeing. Many people incorrectly see the body and the brain apart, with the body being dedicated for action and the brain being dedicated for thinking, feeling, cognition, memory, and sensory functions. On the other hand, the end-goal of the entire human body, including the brain, is aimed at action or movement. The motor system of the brain is a critical facet of physical mobility and mental agility. The brain has a huge memory of prior knowledge, and every moment it keeps receiving new data as new sensory inputs. The brain has the intrinsic wonderful capacity to combine both to trigger a motor control mechanism that can physically display itself as an ultimate movement, which could be one of the following: verbal talk, body language, writing, or typing, and physical movement. It is important to understand that the speed and the specificity of the brain to store, retrieve, and analyse memory on one hand, and to receive and analyse new data inputs on the other hand leads to the agility of the brain. There is, however, a big catch. The set of beliefs, some positive and some negative, some action-oriented and some inaction-oriented, stifle or speed up, and distort or reinforce the motor control mechanism of the brain, influencing the ultimate agility of the brain to act proactively or reactively. The above illustrates that the agility of the brain is a function of not only knowledge and sensitivity, which must be at high levels, but also of the beliefs that must be appropriate to the situation.

There is, however, one more paradigm that influences the agility: the feedback mechanism. Every movement of the type mentioned above leads to a new sensation; the brain always has a prediction of the intended response. The ability of the brain to sensitively receive the physical response and read the actual response determines the effectiveness of the feedback mechanism. Here again, the set of beliefs one has about people, circumstances, and outcomes influences the effectiveness of the feedback mechanism. The outcomes of each of the feedback experiences go into the memory bank. There is, of course, the importance of sleep in the agility of the brain. A well-rested brain is an optimally agile brain. A sleep-deprived brain is a negative influence not only on physical mobility and mental agility but also on lifespan itself.

It is unfortunate that not much attention is paid by organizations and individuals on enabling the personalization of sleep as a daily prophylactic essential medicine that each person needs to have. In the absence of that, individuals tend to adopt erroneous models of sleep (often benchmarking with other individuals), with unknown adverse influences on the motor ability and the mental agility. Organizations treat sleep as a wholly personal issue. Whether such a position is correct or not, organizations must at least design and guide the employee work patterns such that employees are able to have a fair measure of sleep every day. By the same token, employees must voice their concerns if they are deprived of reasonable sleep because of continuous work pressures. Figure 9.2 is a framework of the mobile body and agile mind.

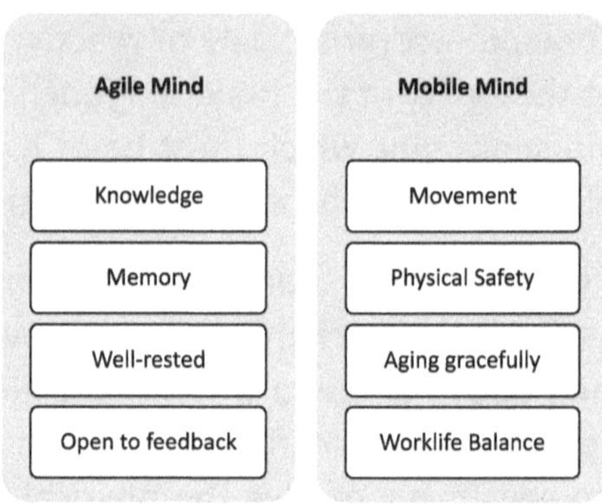

Figure 9.2: A Framework of Mobile Body and Agile mind

Mobile Body with Agile Brain

This chapter has drawn attention to the fact that a wholesome life that is enabled by a mobile body, and an agile mind is essential for a fulfilling life. There is a larger challenge in understanding the interdependence and synergy that exist in the mobility of body and the agility of the mind in the context of a wholesome life. At present, there is an enormous understanding of the physical attributes and kinetics of the human body. Though much less understood, the secrets of the brain are also being unravelled at a fast clip. Unfortunately, individuals view the knowledge, even if expressed in layman's language, as a subject of medicine rather as a valuable component of active living. The interrelationship between physical mobility and mental agility needs an even greater appreciation. The prescription for wholesome living is in one's own hands. This chapter cannot obviously deal with all the associated factors that have certain fundamental importance to the two goals; factors such as food and nutrition, lifestyle and exercise, and emotional stability support the two goals enormously; very importantly, the gut is now known to have a more substantial impact on the overall health, including brain health, than considered earlier.

The world observes several days earmarked for human health, including World Heart Day. Newspapers provide valuable information on exercise and nutrition, among others, that helps maintain a healthy heart and body and live happily. The information also contains warnings on the deleterious impact of alcoholism and smoking on the human wellbeing. If nothing else, alcoholism and smoking adversely influence mobility and agility. Yet, we see the twin temptations of alcoholism and smoking simply not going away from the society. There are, of course, several other person-specific detractors of good health such as carbohydrates, sugar, salt, oil, fats and gluten. Processed and hyper processed foods have an overdose of these factors. Governing one's life through these and other "gifts" of modern, instant living is truly a complex challenge. The only way to address the complexity is to have a simple all-encompassing objective of a wholesome life, whether at work or off work, and achieve it through a synergistic combination of a mobile body and an agile brain. Beyond the God-given DNA, this requires a carefully cultivated Indian dietary nutrition Ayurveda (IDNA). In a climate when the ancient, time-tested Indian vegetarian food system is under threat owing to modernization and westernization through processed and hyper processed instant and convenience foods, the society, at least in India, requires an IDNA revolution much like the famous green revolution and the white revolution that transformed the agriculture and dairy scenarios respectively in India.

Chapter 10

Knowledge and Strategy

Many young people, as they embark upon their educational and experience journeys, are often intrigued, and stymied in their analysis of what kind of focus and/or versatility in their journeys would provide them with appropriate career growth and satisfaction. There cannot be easy answers to this query as the variables that influence one's career development go beyond education and experience. That said, education and experience are two of the most profound variables that influence a person and his or her contributions to any system. Education and experience not only add knowledge on a continuous basis but also influence personality development.

Any template that helps the aspirants to understand themselves and their career ecosystem better should be a welcome addition to management and organizational literature. The template cannot be about which educational course or industry domain is better or worse from a career point of view. The template must be more generic and independent of such choices. The oriental model advocates specialization in education and experience; it almost frowns upon darting across streams. The western model is open to, and even welcomes, versatility in education and experience. Alternatives are possible when a matrix approach is taken, covering education and experience through the filters of specialization and diversification. An individual's breadth and depth of competencies are reflected through the interplay of these four factors.

Four Categories

Fundamentally, there are four options for an individual with respect to education or experience. He or she can pursue specialization or diversification during education (represented by knowledge). She can also pursue specialization or diversification in an industry of employment. Individuals can, therefore, be slotted in one of the four quadrants of the education–experience matrix. These are (i) Knowledge Specialization–Experience Specialization (KSES), (ii) Knowledge Diversification–Experience Specialization (KDES), (iii) Knowledge Specialization–Experience Diversification (KSED), and (iv) Knowledge Diversification–Experience Diversification (KDED). For ease of reference and for representative reflection, these four categories of individuals may be referred to as Mountaineers, Miners, Seafarers and Explorers, respectively. The nomenclature is supported logically as further discussed below.

The individual who specializes in a particular education stream and sticks to a particular related industry domain is very much like a mountaineer who masters mountaineering and is clear about the singular mountain he needs to climb; hence KSES individuals are best named as Mountaineers. The individual who diversifies into many educational streams but sticks to a particular industry domain is quite like a miner who masters multiple mining technologies to find that best metal or mineral; hence KDES individuals are appropriately named as Miners. The individual who specializes in one educational stream but diversifies into many industry domains is like a sailor who trusts his ship to navigate through the varied seas; hence KSED individuals are logically named as Seafarers. The individual who diversifies into many educational streams and diversifies into multiple industry settings is like an explorer who constantly learns and embraces the new to achieve the prize catch; hence KDED individuals are reasoned to be Explorers. Figure 10.1 presents a matrix of education, experience, specialization, and diversification.

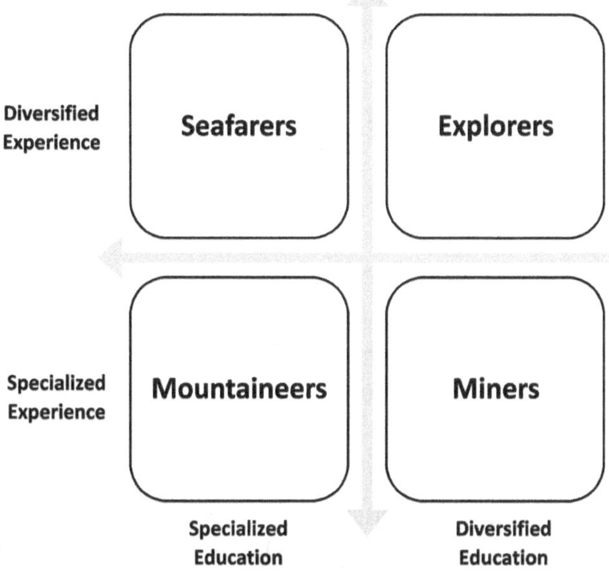

Figure 10.1: Education-Experience-Specialization-Diversification Matrix

1. The Successful Mountaineer (KSES Executive)

To be a successful Mountaineer in the professional or corporate world, one must have a strong aptitude for the subject or domain and a commitment to contribute through a synergy of academic knowledge and practical experience in the industry. A good example would be a basic degree in mechanical engineering, followed by a postgraduate degree in automobile engineering or other specializations such as thermal engineering, metal forming, robotics, or mechatronics and a career in an automobile firm. Typically, he or she would commence the career in one of the three core areas of product development, manufacture, or marketing and move on to become a functional head and eventually a business head. The linkage of education and experience with the subject and domain aptitude is the hallmark of the successful Mountaineer.

To be a successful career Mountaineer, the professional executive would need to have all the technique and patience of the real mountaineer. The career path for a person specialized in and dedicated to a particular domain, industry, and even a company is likely to be challenging with slow growth and slippery terrain. It requires a perfection of subject knowledge and conversion of knowledge into results to become differentiated. Automotive, aerospace, and metals as well as engineering majors recruit each year scores of graduate engineers suited to different functions, and only a handful can reach the top. It is, however, a feasible target illustrated by the likes of Alan Mulally of Boeing and Ford and A. M. Naik of L&T, and several other graduate engineers who reached the top in their respective industries. It pays to be a Mountaineer if education and experience are aligned, with aptitude serving as the glue.

2. The Successful Miner (KDES Executive)

The successful Miner in the professional or corporate world is like a miner in search of precious metals and minerals. He is likely to be highly career focused, and motivated to reach the top by being as broad spectrum as possible in terms of functional capabilities. An individual who pursues a graduate degree in any engineering discipline, followed by a postgraduate degree in business management or a professional who completes chartered accountancy, company secretaryship, and cost accounting courses is driven by an ambition to mine wider and grow faster, picking prize assignments and seeking functional adjacencies in growth. As opposed to the Mountaineer who has committed aptitude, the Miner tends to have flexibility and adaptability as the key drivers.

To be a successful Miner, the professional or corporate executive needs to have, like the real-life miner, a fine discriminating and refining power. Knowing more subjects or dabbling in multiple disciplines is not necessarily a sure passport to the top. Successful move to the top is often based on some solid achievements in certain core functional or business areas. The uniqueness of knowing multiple domains must be reflected in an ability to define, plan, and execute for strategic goals, with greater end-to-end connectivity. Many senior executives at the top in an industry conform to the pattern of learning more and contributing singularly to a specialized industry. Indian industry and Indian executives appear to prefer the Miner model.

3. The Successful Seafarer (KSED Executive)

The successful Seafarer has an aptitude for, and a belief in, his core subjects just as the successful real-life sailor has control on, and confidence in, his ship. He is also not easily laid off by the vastness of practical applications that his core specialization can explore. Examples of this type of career planning relate to educational specializations that are not industry-specific, and instead are industry-neutral. Specializations like finance, information technology, law, electronics, and instrumentation that can find scope and need in any industry are the typical Seafarer's preferences. However, certain gritty Seafarers are wont to use their educational specializations in uncharted seas of radically different industries. Unlike the Mountaineer who has a certain natural alignment of education and experience and the Miner who has a vast functional spread for a unitary industry, the Seafarer has a major challenge. The Seafarer's knowledge specialization must result in such notable contributions that could help him or her become positioned for growth in competition with Mountaineers and Miners that are bound to exist in an organization.

To be a successful Seafarer, the individual must have the innovative ability to apply his specialization to achieve competitive advantage for any industry. He or she also should have the competitive and tenacious spirit to push the envelope and create new areas of contribution to the industry. An instrumentation engineer would, for example, be able to secure new levels of automation for any industry. A finance professional can bring her vast core and collateral functional knowledge to lead the company in any industry to newer levels of financial solidity, costing sharpness, overseas listing, and so on. In addition, a Seafarer would need to have an extra set of behavioural competencies to be seen as a strategic manager despite strong functional specialization. If the Seafarer does not possess or acquire such soft skills, it is quite possible that a Seafarer would remain a knowledge worker or a subject expert even in the long term; this, however, need not necessarily be a bad outcome either for the individual or the organization!

4. *The Successful Explorer (KDED Executive)*

There could be a view that an Explorer would end up as a rolling stone, gathering no mass in the sober, steady corporate and organizational worlds. On the other hand, the Explorer represents the quintessential Gen-Next executive, eager to absorb multiple subjects and dabble in several domains. She is also eager and motivated to constantly search for an organizational home that not merely meets her expectations but challenges her to explore higher trajectories. The new-age young CEOs and the young entrepreneurs proposing new ideas are the representatives of the Explorer category. Some Explorers tend to become turnaround specialists and growth drivers. Most Explorers also become highly successful as consultants with diversified competencies and organizational deliveries.

To be successful, the Explorer needs to be an intensely absorbing person, linking subject mastery and organizational delivery to each moment's challenge rather than to the nature of degrees or longevity in organizations. The Explorer tends to have a bit of the Mountaineer, Miner, and Seafarer characteristics in her but according to his own "mix and match" capability. The Explorer is characterized essentially by lateral thinking and an ability to generate new thinking from current situations and adapt past experiences to new situations. Explorers eventually make excellent heads of diversified business conglomerates, and not surprisingly highly successful bureaucrats and public servants. Business stalwarts like J. R. D. Tata and Ratan Tata are legendary examples. Figure 10.2 summarizes the above four executive typologies in terms of six factors.

Executive Type	**The Successful Mountaineer**	**The Successful Miner**	**The Successful Seafarer**	**The Successful Explorer**
Career Orientation	High	High	High	High
Subject Knowledge	High on hard skills	Diverse	High on soft skills	Lateral thinking skills
Result Orientation	High, mono task	High, multitask	Excels in uncharted territories	Excels in uncertain areas
Diligence	High	High	High	High
Passion	High	High	High	High
Focus	Singular, goal driven	Adaptive to opportunities	Pushes the envelope in all navigable routes	Open to all possibilities

Figure 10.2: The Four Executive Typologies

Talent–Organization Matrix

An ideal organizational format of a growing organization would offer adequate space for all the four classes of performers—the Mountaineers, the Miners, the Seafarers, and the Explorers. Diversified companies organized in terms of business units offer much greater space for all the four classes of aspirants. That said, their existence or requirement is also contextual. If an organization chooses to be specialized and narrowly focused, it will need, and tend to have, more Mountaineers. If an organization is narrowly focused but needs new ideas to propel turnaround or growth, it will need and tend to have more Miners. If an organization is in search of a core competence, it will need, and tend to have, Seafarers. If an organization needs diversification, or is already a business conglomerate, it will need, and tend to have Explorers.

The above has important implications for strategy formulation and talent management at the corporate level and the choice of a company and career at the individual level. There has been a debate whether structure or strategy precedes the other, and the debate has been settled with the validated hypothesis that structure follows strategy. The discussion in this chapter also leads to a debate whether strategy sets the talent needs or talent helps create a sustainable strategy. Potentially, a broad vision for the organization should lead to the induction of an appropriate mix of Mountaineers, Miners, Seafarers, and Explorers that can develop and execute a required strategy. Young aspirants need to understand that when they choose their unique educational paths and experience pathways, they are not only categorizing themselves into one of the four classes but are also developing themselves into human dynamos that can power organizations in potentially unique ways.

Chapter 11

Skill and Career Development

Young people regardless of their educational streams are restless to discover the elixir of professional growth. Each educational stream by virtue of the unique nature of its domain imbues in its students' certain unique capabilities. Literature, for example, provides its students with an ability to appreciate the dynamics of humans and nature. Commerce makes its students aware of the worth of trade and business. Accounting makes students proficient in the deployment and measurement of assets and liabilities. Science makes its students create the bridge between the natural and synthetic—the organic and inorganic. Engineering teaches its students the ability to convert ideas into gadgets—the abstract into real. In a similar manner, each professional course that has a technical characteristic of its own provides unique characteristics to the students.

Doubtless, these professional courses help individuals enter organizations and functions of their choice and grow in their careers based on further professional specialization or diversification. It is not, however, so well established that educational excellence by itself provides the motive force for managerial and leadership development. If technical capabilities as embedded through professional courses are reinforced with soft skills such as communication, interpersonal, and other behavioural skills, it would help individuals achieve higher goals through superior performance. While a combination of such hard skills and soft skills is undoubtedly very much needed, there is a more fundamental skill set that enables truly superior competitive performance. This chapter proposes a model that is a combination of conceptual, analytical, technical, creative, and holistic capabilities. The CATCH Capabilities model, illustrated in Figure 11.1, is discussed below.

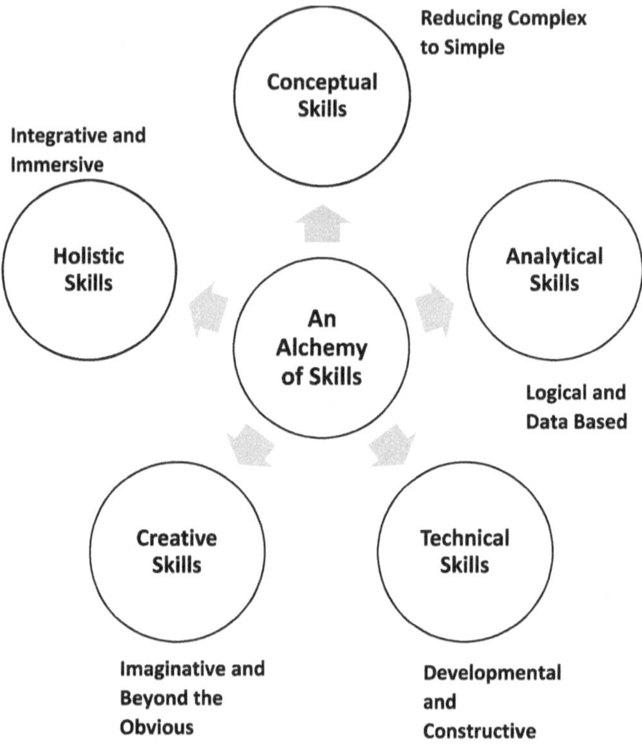

Figure 11.1: A Framework of Five Core Skills

Conceptual

Simplistically, conceptual skills are ideation or imagination skills. In a managerial sense, they represent the skills that help an individual crystallize complex and abstract problems in terms of core themes and ideas. An insightful conceptual positioning could stem from how companies view their products – as low-cost products or low-price products. Similarly, firms may conceptually position their products based on either price or value. The conceptual clarity on costs and prices teaches us that fundamentally the firm must be a low-cost operation whereupon it can automatically be a real low-fare firm if it chooses to; it could well choose to be a high-price and high-margin firm. Another exemplary conceptualization was experienced by me when a Director of an Indian Institute of Management (IIM) told the professors at an Indian Institute of Technology (IIT) struggling to dissect the pros and cons of having a management school within the IIT that it would be like having a mini-IIM in the IIT campus, implying that it is a cultural issue.

Conceptual thinking enables a leader or a manager to understand the core opportunities and challenges facing a business; it cuts out clutter. It helps managers and leaders avoid distractions. Conceptual thinking is particularly helpful when firms are either in the start-up or end-state phase of business or when they are faced with strategic crossroads. The uncertainty of future options and the unpredictability of data points are managed by the conceptual definition of the core problems. A firm that has a product lead time of five years and has been paralyzed from investments for five years can be conceptually concluded to have lost a decade of life and several decades of competitive advantage, even without any data analysis. Equally, such a company can be conceptually held to be capable of re-entering the competitive game with only a clever acquisition. Conceptual thinking simplifies the otherwise complex business life.

Analytical

Analytical skills are those that enable an individual use a logical method of thinking about anything to understand it, especially by looking at all the constituent parts separately. It typically deploys scientific and research-based approaches. The link between conceptual and analytical skills is simple; the analytical part can take off optimally once the conceptual part is clear. Taking the cost–price example, once conceptual clarity is established that low cost rather than low price is the right model on a fundamental basis, analytics would need to focus on how the lowest cost of a product with the desired quality level could be achieved. This would involve analysing every component of the cost structure for frugality and every component of customer service for value optimality. The more comprehensive the analysis is, the better would be the operating model. That said, analytics without conceptual crystallization would be a wild goose chase.

Analysis provides choices and generates data points that would help managements make appropriate decisions. Conceptual clarity would continue to help in making analysis better. For example, the layering of additional fares on a base fare cannot be good analytics; so is the case with the complex dynamic fare model. The model develops in an opaque manner a high average fare for the airliner, leveraging the seductive promotional advance fares and exploitative usurious last-day fares. Such a model, however, would not be in keeping with the concept of a true low-cost airliner that is expected to provide maximal perceived service with minimal absorbed cost to the common citizen. Analytics requires a sound business background; analysts should understand the vital–essential–desirable as well as the fundamental–core–peripheral concepts as appropriate to the industry or the business one is in. Analysts should also appreciate where what tools would be relevant; operations research, for example, would be applicable for route planning, whereas game theory could be relevant for competitor analysis and simple arithmetic appropriate for standard costing.

Technical

Although considered allied to, or reflective of, engineering and technology, technical skills have a broader connotation as well. Any skill required for a person to perform a job efficiently and effectively is a technical skill. Technical skill typically grows out of the knowledge of a subject and is the fundamental core knowledge to be in a domain or lead it. Every business requires several technical skills; what is a core technical skill for one industry could be an enabler for another industry. For example, for an automobile firm, design and manufacturing technology would be the core domain while finance and IT would be supportive technical domains. For a banking firm, finance and IT would be core while civil engineering would be supportive. Regardless of such differentiation, technically one must be an expert in one's domain. Companies such as GE and Unilever focus on multifunctional expertise to build themselves into firms with a sustainable competitive advantage.

Technical skills are acquired through serious curricular efforts, proactive extracurricular reading, and intense on-the-job deployment and learning. Technical skills are reinforced by continuous learning; it is more than a simple learning curve effect. A doctor or a surgeon continuously adds to his or her medical skills through each case he or she handles. A maintenance engineer continuously adds to his or her preventive maintenance capability with every breakdown maintenance case he or she handles. A product designer continuously improves his or her products by observing customer usage and integrating material and other technologies. An accountant understands the power of numbers and their implications by continuously monitoring global accounting regulations and trends for generally accepted accounting practices of different countries, and related case laws. Being constantly studious is the only way to acquire and enhance technical skills.

Creative

Creative skill involves the use of skill and imagination to produce a new work in any domain, be it a work of art, science, or engineering. Many experts consider that creativity and originality are even more important than technical skill. If an airliner can creatively transport its employees seamlessly across the nation through a hub-and-spoke strategy, it would provide competitive differentiation. If a full-fare airliner can provide an online air ticket reservation and purchase facility with anytime access without dynamic fares, compatible with any type of device, it could nurture for itself a creative niche. If an airliner can replace its in-flight print magazine by a digital version displayed on individual screens, it can not only reduce costs but also provide the whole archive of magazines to information lovers. If the ground handling of cargo and passengers, and the housekeeping and maintenance of aircraft are improved to reduce vehicle turnaround in airports by 50%, an airline could add one additional flight to its daily schedule. By opening its own dedicated takeaway food kiosk in the departure terminal, an airline can save on crimped up and inadequate service on its flights, more particularly the short-haul ones.

Creativity differentiates the winners from the losers, more so the sustainable growth firms from the also-rans. Creativity requires an independent and questioning mind that constantly seeks improvements at one level and out-of-the-box thinking at another level. Creative skill comes with constant observation but each time with a fresh enquiring eye and an agile problem-solving mind. Creativity essentially comes with discovering invisible problems, finding new ways of solving difficult problems, and fulfilling customer needs in better manner—the hallmarks of start-up activity as well. The process of technological development is based on creativity. Creativity can come from knowledge or from practice. The former should lead one to find better ways from knowledge. The latter should lead to a quest for knowledge that can improve practice. Many times, small but focused experiments become scalable for global impact. Creative payment gateways, for example, have revolutionized global online commerce and fund transfers. A creative patient record management system can revolutionize national healthcare registry, as another example. Successful start-ups develop from creative operational or business solutions.

Holistic

Holistic skill is the ability to consider a whole thing or being to be more than a collection of parts. Holistic life and holistic medicine are examples of common phraseologies of holism. Holism is the philosophical approach that the whole, of anything, must be considered to understand its different parts. Holism is one of the most complex capabilities to possess because it is a multidimensional attribute covering all overt and latent characteristics, direct and indirect influencers, and current and future evolutions. Reverting to the airline example, the business plan of a low-cost airline involving important parameters such as fleet mix, route network, schedule density, and several other factors are dependent on the nature of airport infrastructure in various cities and towns. It would be segmented thinking to buy large capacity aircraft and hope to connect all the tier 2 and tier 3 cities; it would not work as a holistic strategy because the short runways would not accept such larger aircraft. It would be somewhat like an international airline like Lufthansa planning to convert its entire fleet to A 380 (the largest aircraft) even though only few global cities can accommodate such wide-bodied aircraft.

Holism requires thinking and imagining beyond the obvious, connecting the visible and invisible dots of the industry boundary, industry value map, and inflection points in regulatory evolution. This is not necessarily the forte of only the wise elderly or apex leaders; all individuals who can process multiple sets of data and information and form patterns can develop a holistic approach to what they seek to accomplish. Holism is a temporally integrative capability as well; it involves an ability to connect the certain past, volatile present, and uncertain future to achieve a holistic solution. It merges emotion with objectivity, and experience with anticipation to create a new paradigm that others less endowed would find difficult to mimic. Holism requires that the four skills discussed earlier, namely conceptual, analytical, technical, and creative are well developed in an individual. Holism in such individuals acts as a capstan capability.

The CATCH

If these constitute the five virtuous capabilities for personality, knowledge, and leadership development, it must be intriguing that such programs emphasize only some of the capabilities; for example, analytical and technical capabilities are the most emphasized. The reason lies in the belief that while analytical and technical skills can be "taught and acquired," the other three skills are dependent on how the brain is hardwired with respect to conceptualization, creativity, and holism. This could be a catch in adopting the conceptual, analytical, technical, creative, and holistic (CATCH) development model on a wider scale; but the catch is more imaginary than real! As with many developmental activities, introspection, on the part of the developer and the developing person (the mentor and the mentee, the guru and sishya, the boss and the subordinate, the teacher and the student, the leader and the follower, as the case may be). Fundamentally, the developer should be a CATCH personality to develop the individuals, and needless to add, even the developers would need to develop themselves to make the CATCH development template work. Figure 11.2 illustrates, through the example of electric vehicles, how CATCH can be applied even to a mammoth game-changing developmental activity.

Skill Type	Activity/ Outcome
Conceptual	• Imagine non-fossil fuel vehicles to cut down pollution • Imagine self-driving cars to enhance safety and productivity on roads
Analytical	• Analyze and identify electric vehicles as the best possible solution • Analyze imaging, computer and sensor-aided approaches
Technological	• Re-engineer batteries and vehicles to suit the new requirements • Develop battery charging technologies • Develop newer battery materials
Creative	• Develop battery-swapping as a balance between power and range for optimal mobility • Reconfigure driving and ownership practices for seamless mobility • Establish national charging infrastructure collaboratively
Holistic	• Connect and reconfigure the whole spectrum of vehicle makers, component makers, material manufacturers, charge providers, power suppliers and automobile users to develop a total electric vehicle ecosystem

Figure 11.2: Application of CATCH for Electric Vehicles

Chapter 12

Data Analytics and Decisive Execution

Progress is the essence of life. Progress is based on certain fundamentals. These are: destination, path, and execution. Each journey when completed must lead to the next progress journey. These journeys must be undertaken with a clear understanding of the competencies and resources required. Not many can develop these guideposts by themselves with due introspection, reflection, and ownership. Everyone is subject to myriad influences from families, friends, institutions, and societies. To cap it all, very few have the philosophical approach to appreciate progress and take in their stride any regress.

Most people tend to have a feeling of having failed to progress as much as one should have; only the shades vary across the rich and poor. Ironically, the distress about lacks or inadequacy of progress increases with increasing prosperity while blind acceptance of status quo seems to deepen with increasing poverty. These and various other related socio-economic and socio-philosophic considerations are extremely complex, and do not easily lend themselves to a simple macro analysis or a macro solution. Individuals even in their own spaces of competencies and aspirations struggle with issues of progress and satisfaction. Factors as simple as destination, path and execution defy clear mastery by even people with a high level of intellectual capability. The human brain is continuously subject to triggers of speedup and slowdown that continuously make individuals accelerate or vacillate in their journeys of progress in a life that poses multiple options.

Accelerators and Vacillators

Life is marked by change with its own velocity and periodic acceleration. The accelerators are partly wired in one's personality (for example, get rich quickly, climb up the social ladder fast, win laurels repeatedly, take risks to grow fast, and so on) but also require environmental triggers (for example, a new start-up culture, a new savings and investment ecosystem, more attractive financial instruments, an aggressive family environment, and so on). When these factors, part internal and part external, align for an individual, the destination, path, and progress tend to be clear. Doubtless, there would be speed breakers on the way, but the accelerators have their inbuilt momentum to overcome the hurdles. The downside would stem occasionally from the adventurous nature that fails to distinguish between speed breakers that are mere cautions and those that are precursors to dead-end points.

Vacillation is the threat to acceleration in the journey of life. It is a result of confusion or lack of clarity in one's mind. Vacillation as much as steadfastness, and confusion as much as clarity are normal human tendencies because of the way everyone is wired in terms of one's personality (for example, risk-averse, self-satisfied, and so on) and the way the external environment tends to project short-term disappointments as long-term distress (for example, volatility in commodity prices, job market trends, and so on). When these internal and external factors combine for an individual, the destination and path would appear to be hazy and progress tardy. Doubtless, there would be compelling pressures to gain traction on account of socioeconomic benchmarks, but the inherent trend of vacillators would make a person to procrastinate rather than decide. In fact, the matrix of deliberation and decisiveness can be utilized by accelerators and vacillators alike to overcome their inherent weaknesses and reinforce their strengths.

Deliberation and Decisiveness

To solve the puzzle, individuals need to be scaled on the two dimensions of deliberation and decisiveness. These two dimensions are commonly seen to be inherently contra to each other. An individual who is least deliberative may tend to be quickly decisive while an individual who is extremely deliberative may tend to be least decisive. This is a simplistic view. Individuals tend to be on a scale of low to high on deliberation as well as on decisiveness. Besides, not in all cases there would be any correlation, positive or inverse, between the two variables. Individuals must carefully develop themselves on the deliberation–decisiveness matrix. There would be four groups of individuals: (i) Low Deliberators–Quick Deciders, (ii) High Deliberators–Slow Deciders, (iii) Low Deliberators–Slow Deciders, and (iv) High Deliberators–Quick Deciders. Clearly, a presence in the group (iv) is something to be aimed at. Figure 12.1 represents a typical deliberation–decisiveness matrix.

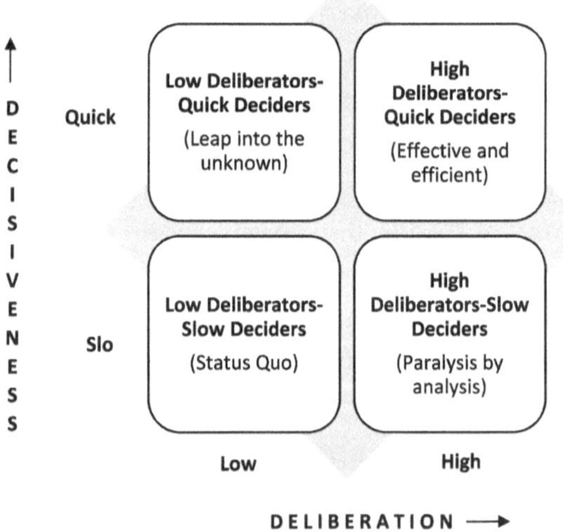

Figure 12.1: Deliberation–Decisiveness Matrix

While lack of deliberation is not healthy, excessive deliberation without quick decision-making is counterproductive. High deliberation in this context means consideration of all aspects in an optimum time frame rather than an endless thinking process. Low deliberation means not deliberating enough or deliberating too quickly. While being a slow decider is not a virtue if the slowness is due to high deliberations, it is probably next to the best. Obviously, being a low deliberator and quick decider would lead to unhealthy choices. Being a low deliberator and slow decider is also a sure recipe for a skewed and frozen life. Being high on deliberations and simultaneously being quickly decisive gets the best of both the worlds to the individual. Individuals belonging to this group possess and develop a high level of information processing capability. However, the deliberation–decisiveness matrix needs to be further cascaded in terms of linkage between information and deliberation on one hand and decisiveness and implementation on the other. Here again, a matrix approach provides clarity to individuals.

Information and Implementation

Deliberation can only be based on information. In today's Internet-driven world, there is no paucity of information; in fact, one is overwhelmed by data and information. Conversational AI platforms such as ChatGPT provide distilled information and guidance, additionally. The greater the availability of quality information, the greater the possibility of quality deliberation. Even then there is no assured linkage. We can have (i) Low Deliberators–Low Information (this probably is a hapless group!), (ii) Low Deliberators–High Information (this group is handicapped by low information-processing capability), (iii) High Deliberators–Low Information (this group is stuck with procrastination), and (iv) High Deliberators– High Information (this group makes quality analysis and decision-making choices). While information is the core of deliberation, deliberation is the proper precursor to decision-making. Decision-making, of course, is futile without implementation.

Decisiveness is reinforced with implementation capability (also termed execution capability). There is no automatic connection between quick decision-making and speedy implementation. The former is largely an individual phenomenon requiring an ability to analyse the self and the environment, whereas the latter is a leadership capability requiring an ability to understand, lead, and manage others. Here again, a matrix approach would be helpful. We can have (i) Slow Deciders–Slow Implementers, (ii) Quick Deciders–Slow Implementers, (iii) Slow Deciders–Quick Implementers, and (iv) Quick Deciders–Quick Implementers. The first group clearly is the non-starter group in today's competitive world, whereas the second group, though blessed with a quick start, is a losing proposition. The third group makes up for procrastinated decision-making with quick implementation. The fourth group is the truly competitive group excelling in both decisiveness and implementation.

Pathway to Progress

The above discussion leads us to the conclusion that one should be a member of three conceptual groups to make meaningful progress. Fundamentally, one should be a high deliberator and quick decider. This enables a higher quality of decision with a faster go-to-market possibility. High deliberation, however, should stem from a capability to process a high amount of information. Quick decision-making, likewise, should be followed through and reinforced by an ability to quickly implement. As compared to this virtuous grouping of three, there tend to be nine other groupings that are suboptimal or even counterproductive. The odds of placing oneself, naturally or effortlessly, in the superior grouping are statistically low, requiring that individuals need to understand the true meaning and the essential relevance of deliberation, information, decisiveness, and implementation as the four components of an accelerated journey of progress in life, and resolutely develop themselves to be in that virtuous quadrant.

Interestingly, decision-making happens only periodically, and implementation follows with a specific time horizon (not to be whimsically changed). This applies equally to a student's educational path or a businessman's industrial path. However, the flow of information and, therefore, the triggers for deliberation occur rather continuously for any individual in any play of life. It is important to keep the deliberation process perpetually on but manage it in such a way that it does not confuse a person and make the path of progress a meandering one. For those who manage this balance in the deliberation, information, decisiveness, and implementation model on an ongoing basis, success comes naturally and logically. It is, however, amazing to see how even intellectually capable people become thwarted on their paths of progress. As discussed in this chapter, there could be an explanation of that too. Those who are mindful and thoughtful of the digressions would still be successful. Figure 12.2 represents the information–deliberation matrix as discussed.

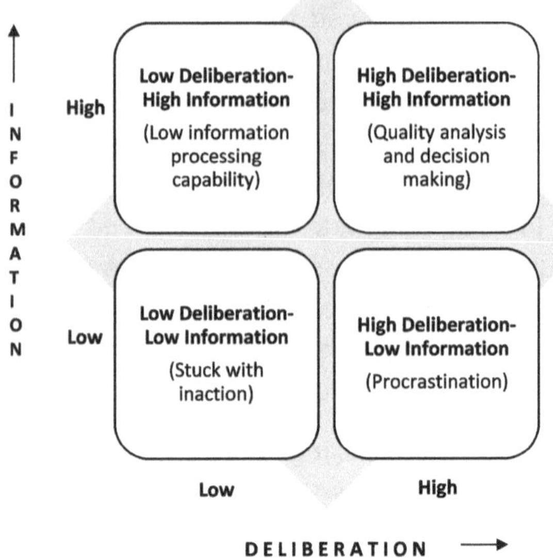

Figure 12.2: Information–Deliberation Matrix

In summary, the ability of an individual to manage information, deliberation, and decisiveness in combinations determines the influencing capability of the individual.

Chapter 13

Aligned Action

Thoughts are generally irrepressible. Expressions and actions, in contrast, are relatively controllable. There can be no expression or action without thought. Even in involuntary actions, some system or the other of the body "thinks." The world expects all expressions and actions to be well-thought-out. A spiritual guru said that a blow from one person to another person can heal with time but an abuse or indictment from one to another would never heal even with time. That is the power of the word, he said. The physiological and neurological basis of thoughts and speech is a complex field of study. It is rational and evidence-based; it can be studied with behavioural observations of a person or scanning of the person's brain. That said, every thought–expression–action (TEA) linkage is neither spontaneous nor unpredictable; it is conditioned, by one's own learnings and experiences as well as expectations.

Societies that are naturally evolved but with fractious human agglomerations and organizations that are synthetically established with heterogenous employees require conditioned behaviour in terms of thoughts, expressions, and actions. Without conditioned behaviour, societies and organizations would be at risk of disruption, if not chaos. However, completely conditioned behaviour robs the societies and organizations of the principal benefit of human existence—creativity and innovation. The need for balance between spontaneity (hence of creativity and innovation) and moderation (hence of order and discipline) is genuine for societies and organizations but quite difficult to achieve. Individuals, as they mature and develop the abilities of reflection and introspection, can help promote positive conditioned behaviour. Figure 13.1 illustrates the human behavioural cycle.

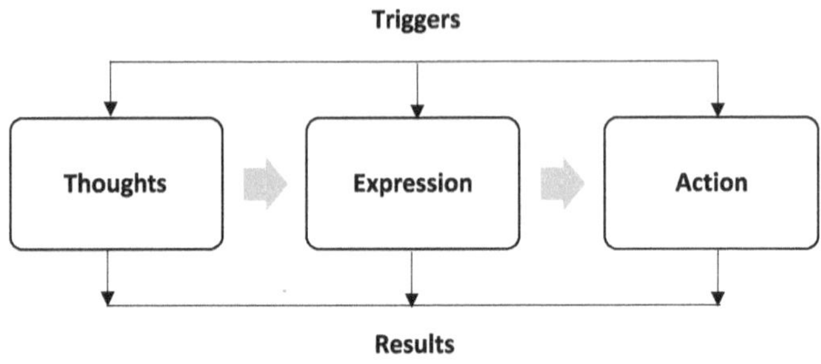

Figure 13.1: The Human Behavioural Cycle

Cluttering, Decluttering

Human beings are processors of abundant information. Even when they are not in conversation with fellow beings, their ecosystems tend to be in conversation with them. These conversations, whether active or passive, shape the thoughts of the individuals. These thoughts, as they bubble up, set in motion a complex chain of feedback mechanisms. Left uncontrolled, a person's mind could become an uncontrolled cauldron of thoughts. Mercifully, a few things help control the phenomenon. Firstly, a person's innate ability to moderate the thought processes helps. Secondly, a preference for positive thoughts results in a helpful cycle of positive expressions, positive feedback, positive actions, and positive recognitions. Thirdly, as a person moves from the thought and expression phases to the action phase, he or she becomes focused, and goal directed. For example, a person in search of an accommodation to buy would be subject to multiple thoughts in the exploration phase but becomes focused on house construction once he narrows down the choice to a particular acquisition.

There are four other important means to declutter oneself of the unending assault of thoughts. One is the daily natural phenomenon of sleep. Modern research has re-established the age-old philosophy that a healthy period of daily sleep is the best means for rejuvenation of the body and mind. The second is the discipline of daily exercise that brings focus and endurance to the body and mind. The third is the following of a healthy and nutritious diet pattern. The fourth is the ancient practice of yoga and meditation that helps one to become calm and relaxed as well as focused and attentive. The Art of Living Foundation lists several benefits of meditation (http://www.artofliving.org/meditation/meditation-for-you/benefitsof-meditation). The Foundation observes that meditation is like a seed, which when cultivated with care, blossoms to the general wellbeing of a person. Despite the availability of such compelling evidence, people are unable to implement the moderation, focus, and execution trilogy for smart professional work and the sleep, exercise, diet, and meditation framework for healthy personal life.

Starting Early

The NDA government despite its preoccupation with economic reforms and acceleration of economic growth has focused on some important softer aspects of life that need to be imbibed from the early childhood stage. In one of his regular radio addresses, Mann ki Baat, Prime Minister Shri Narendra Modi advised students taking the Class X and Class XII Board examinations that each student should learn to develop faith in oneself as Swami Vivekananda exhorted decades ago and take the examinations as a game to play and learn to relax. He advised students to learn Pranayama or practice Surya Namaskar to reduce stress. In a proud moment for India, the United Nations, on December 10, 2014, adopted June 21 as World Yoga Day, pursuant to Narendra Modi's impassioned plea for yoga in the UN General Assembly in September 2014.

Such guidance and measures should influence the new generation to stay positive from the early years. Like the half-empty or half-full analogy of a drinking glass, it is never too late or too early to start anything positive. There is so much material and expertise that is available in the public domain on sleep–exercise–diet–meditation aspects that it would be inappropriate and inadequate to discuss those aspects in this book. There is, however, less attention and material on the moderation–focus–execution trilogy that is needed in professional life. Within this trilogy again, there is enough literature on keeping focus and driving execution but very little thought on achieving positive moderation in thoughts, expression, and actions. As a result, organizations and societies are focused on conflict management as a discipline of learning and development. A far better route would be to root out the triggers and precursors for conflicts in the thought processes themselves.

Triggers

Achievements, disappointments, targets, goals, teachings, exhortations, criticisms, observations, advice, and a host of other events relating to oneself or others in the society act as triggers for thoughts. Thoughts could vary across a wide spectrum, from mere noting and registering them in memory (or shutting them out of active memory) to feelings of joy or sadness, motivation or inspiration, security or helplessness, introversion, or extroversion, and so on. These, in turn, make individuals to stay satisfied (with the status quo) or become dissatisfied (to change the status quo). The stronger the feelings, the greater would be the triggers. The triggers lead to expressions of satisfaction or dissatisfaction, and later to situations of inaction or action. The intermediate stage of expression between thought and action is important because it provides an opportunity to provide or receive feedback, and thus correct or be corrected.

The intermediate stage of expression is also important because it helps in either dissipation of excessive (often negative) energy or reinforcement for needed (often positive) energy. In certain cases, when the triggers are particularly strong, individuals tend to jump from thought to action directly without going through the very important stage of expression, often leading to undesirable results. While keeping one's own inner counsel does happen, and is also important and appropriate in certain cases, in most situations expression of core thoughts and intended response would go a long way in improving the end results. Needless to add, actions would certainly lead to certain results, which in turn lead to the next cycle of triggers. For one's life to be in a manageable boundary, the triggers for thoughts and the consequent expressions and actions need to be purposeful.

Filters

As one grows up and acquires maturity, the brain or mind starts developing its own filters that are set in place. Typically, an individual consciously or unconsciously passes his or her thoughts, expressions, and actions through these filters. While the triggers add velocity and momentum to one's TEAs, the filters help one to separate the positive ones (or those agreeable to one's personality) from the negative ones (or those disagreeable to one's personality). These filters start the processes of reflection, introspection, evaluation, and selection as the TEAs pass through them. In an ideal situation, only those thoughts that pass through all the filters become expressions and those expressions that pass through all the filters become actions. Developing the right kind of filters and keeping them effective (and unclogged) is certainly in one's capability and helps one in staying TEA positive.

As illustrated in figure 13.2, the typical filters one has in one's mind are the following. The primary one is the emotional filter (will the TEA make me happy or sad, satisfied, or dissatisfied, and motivated or demotivated?). The second is the social filter, social including the family, friends, peers, and the broader society where relevant (will the TEA gain me acceptance or rejection, recognition, or castigation?). The third is the value filter (does the TEA fit into my value system or not?). Only those TEAs that pass through all the three filters make one truly happy. The sequence given above tends to be applicable for a great majority of individuals. For sage and wise individuals, the sequence would probably be in the reverse order: the value filter first followed by the social filter

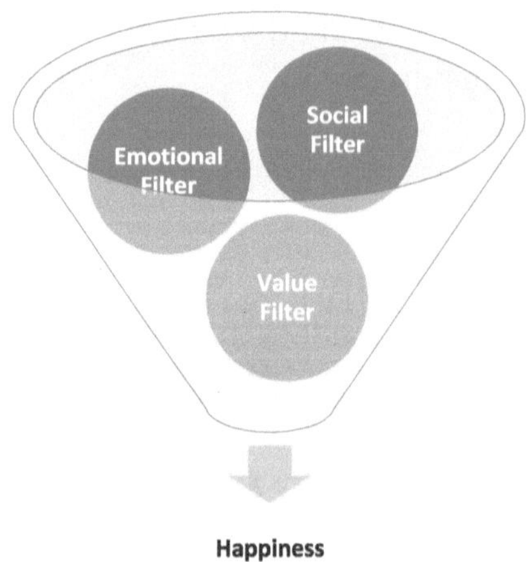

Figure 13.2: Typical Filters One has in One's Mind

and then the emotional filter. While a few other filters like the development filter or the growth filter can be considered, they are also ultimately expressed in terms of emotions. Likewise, while the social filter can be separated into family filter and other filters, it only adds needless complexity.

Staying TEA positive is a worthwhile goal in life. The ability to entertain only positive or agreeable thoughts and ability to declutter one's mind are the fundamental capabilities that help one in the process. The more important aspect is setting the right filters in one's mind. The filters are chosen right and set right depending on one's knowledge of the broader good as may be taught by scriptures, texts, teachers, friends, and families. The social and value filters help one reach alignment and congruence between what is positive and what is agreeable. Staying TEA positive is an organizational possibility and requirement too. From choosing a business to operate in to generating and sharing wealth with stakeholders to fulfilling corporate social responsibility, organizations and corporations have multiple ways to become and stay TEA positive. Organizations that promote a TEA positive culture in their team members would become virtuous organizations. Societies and nations creating ecosystems that help individuals and organizations become TEA positive would become virtuous nations.

Chapter 14

Excelling as Executive

Each generation tends to be more knowledgeable and more aggressive than the previous one. The current generation of job aspirants is no different. If at all, the Internet, social media, and print media have brought globalization and growth on to the forefront. The new generation sees industry and business as a relevant canvas to lay out one's career aspirations. This canvas includes start-up activities as well. This generation also realizes that there is no longer a classic and proven educational or experience paradigm that propels one to the top crust. The bottom of the pyramid that seeks to grow to the top is larger than ever, even as the competition to excel in the process of moving up is fiercer than ever. When an interviewer quizzes on the career goals of a young aspirant, it is now passé for the candidate to say that he or she would perform the best in his or her job and leave the rest to his or her management. Many would even respond that their career goals are nothing less than reaching CEO or CXO positions, the soonest. An aggressiveness or ambition to set the highest goal and then set out a work path is the order of the day. The new-age ambition and nonchalance may be borne out of confidence or casualness. However, if the aspirations are not backed up by achievements, the aspirants as well as the organizations would be in churn. The pathways to growth must, therefore, be well understood in terms of both opportunities and impediments.

Multiple Learning Needs

The roadblock to India's quest for top-of-the-world status, if at all, would be talent or skills shortage. The expectations with which industries and businesses are being set up in India require abundance of the requisite talent with optimal skill-cost balance. Moving beyond the IITs and the IIMs, the broader educational ecosystem must meet, on a wider scale, world-class standards. Talent must lead and not follow industrial developments. Given global competitive pressures, neither India Inc nor the aspiring talent pool can wait for years for a restructured education system to emerge. The available systemic outputs, which may not be fully adequate, must be honed and harnessed to make the best fit of talent and opportunities.

Education, anywhere in the world, does not provide one with readily deployable knowledge. The domains are so varied that no standardized syllabus can meet thousands of work variations. Yet, what education provides is a set of knowledge elements and analytical tools that can be further developed or customized to meet a variety of job needs. It is entirely in the realm of possibility for organizations to leverage the basics to build futures. Similarly, prior experience often teaches many domain fundamentals and process skills that may not be exactly applicable in a new job situation but lay the building blocks. The first job as well as the new job on one hand, and the college fresher as well as the lateral mover all present opportunities that the typical organizational processes in India are ignoring. Rather than blame the educational systems or work environments, employees and employers must focus on multiple learning needs as manifold opportunities emerge in the Indian economy. Figure 14.1 is a pictorial representation of the three organizational growth vectors available for young executives.

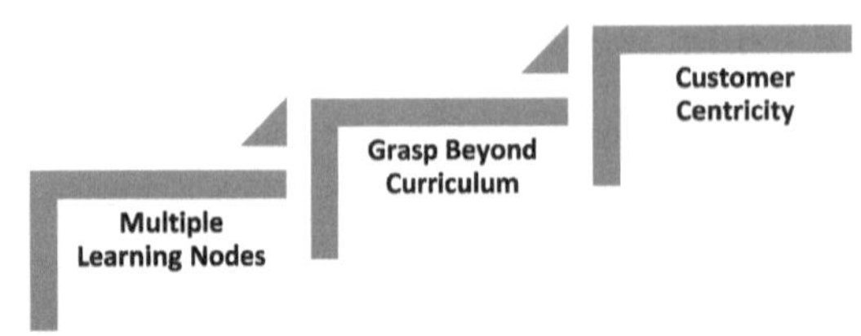

Figure 14.1: The Three Organizational Growth Vectors

Grasp beyond Curriculum

A young executive who aspires to be a chief executive cannot predict for sure if his or her first company would be the home for him as a chief executive too, or if his core domain would continue to be the perfect launch pad for the career journey. It was so for A. M. Naik who joined L&T as a graduate engineer and performed and persevered to become the CEO and chairman of the engineering and construction conglomerate. Others may view A. M. Naik as a role model. Students in India, or even abroad, choose courses based as much on aptitude as by a host of external factors such as demand–supply factors, parental advice, affordability considerations, and vagaries of government policies. While the choice of curriculum may also decide the choice of the first company, there is no set rule that the pathway to career progress is domain-based. There is no such division as technical or non-technical in one's progression to the top. The ability to grasp new knowledge beyond the curriculum together with the ability to apply all knowledge to new applications is the first prerequisite for being on the pathway to a chief executive position.

This is because unlike any other job, the chief executive job requires continuous learning and adaptability to new situations. It is well established that chief executives demonstrate a remarkable capability to go beyond the core curriculum to gain knowledge of new domains. This needs to be a deliberate process-objective of an aspiring executive from the very beginning of the career. Executives who remain devoted to their functions, not bothering about or attempting to learn other functional contours, would be self-cloistered and find it difficult to become multifunction leaders. Organizations when they recruit young executives must focus on their ability for flexible and continuous learning rather than go by only the knowledge–function fit. In many ways, it is necessary for an executive to start a new learning journey once he joins an organization, developing new aptitudes and acquiring new knowledge sets. This does not require that a finance executive should become a physicist or that an engineer should become an accountant to grow in career. The concept of grasp beyond curriculum, however, requires that the executive must understand the drivers of other functions in terms of overall operational and business impact, and the connectivity to his or her core curriculum.

Customer Centricity

This is both an aptitude and a skill. Product- or service-driven organizations are, in fact, customer-centric organizations. Their chief executives convert their personal passion for serving the customers with new products and services into a drive for the creation of innovative products and services. Passion for customer centricity could be built up from the very beginning of one's career. The contemporary organizational value chain comprises not only the three core functions of product development, manufacturing, and marketing but also a host of other functional specializations and sub-specializations that make the core functions deliver optimally. These supportive functions are, for example, quality, regulatory affairs, production planning, corporate planning, business development, information technology, finance, HR, and so on.

In addition, umbrella functions such as environment, safety and health, ethics, compliance, risk management, and CSR determine the values of an organization.

The key to appreciation of customer centricity by a young executive lies in an awareness of how each function, regardless of whether it has a direct interface with the customer or not, has a significant contribution to make for organizations to achieve customer delight. It is easy for young executives to understand how the core functions serve the customers in terms of developing, manufacturing, and selling products. They do not easily understand how they would be serving the customers when their jobs are in other specialized and supportive functions. This is where organizations need to develop the value chain perspective in the young executives. Young executives need to appreciate that quality is a value differentiator, regulatory affairs is a specifications optimizer, production planning is a timely deliverer, corporate planning is a priority balancer, business development is a customer seeker, information technology is a business connector, finance is a resource manager, and human resources is a talent provider. Each of the functional specializations delivers specific value to customers by optimizing the core functions of an organization.

Connected Collaboration

The young executives need to appreciate that customer centricity can be achieved by serving the internal functional customers as well. The ability of a young executive in a function, core or supportive, to connect with internal functions is the foundational component of his or her ability to achieve a mastery of the organizational value chain. It is easier said than done as under the concept of focus and specialization, departments tend to operate as silos in organizations. In such vertically run organizations, departmental managers tend to discourage cross-functional collaboration at the mildest and promote turf wars and interdepartmental politics at the severest. Young executives who acquire and develop value chain perspectives and experiences larger than departmental priorities naturally run a better chance of becoming chief executives. Organizations, and their leaders and managers, have a major responsibility in enabling such a developmental ecosystem. This is also a self-validating and self-fulfilling hypothesis as young executives with such broader perspectives would be the ones to accept and benefit from job rotation programs, thus enriching their careers even further.

Many young executives and chief executives ignore the relevance of, and challenges inherent in, ingraining internal customer orientation as an organizational mindset. The value chain ecosystem needs a broader business understanding and a deeper appreciation of multifunction. Corporations would, therefore, need to provide comprehensive value chain indoctrination to new entrants to establish comprehensive multifunctional appreciation and collaborative cultural moorings in young executives. Departmental managers must eschew the temptation of confining the young entrants to narrow jobs before they understand how they can effectively develop as total organizational personalities, and not merely as cogs in the organizational wheel. To enable this, even organizational design may need to be reinvented. Quite apart from the silo design and operation of departmental units, organizational performance appraisal and reward systems tend to encourage individual performance. Instead, well-designed, and well-operated matrix organizational structures and group incentive schemes linked to collaborative effort are helpful in supporting broader perspectives amongst employees. More fundamental would be the young executives' passion for knowledge acquisition and an organizational culture that promotes a spirit of enquiry.

Ten Essentials

The realization of the concepts of acquiring knowledge outside the core curriculum and native departments is as much dependent on organizational policies and culture as on the young entrants' passion and perseverance. That said, there are ten essential personality goals that young aspirants must keep in mind and assiduously fulfil to become well-rounded executives, justifying a consideration to grow in the organizational hierarchy. These are: respecting higher-order values and ethics, reflecting a persona of trust and transparency, understanding the product-market scope, learning the product and manufacturing intricacies, appreciating the importance of time, integrating a culture of continuous improvement, establishing a level of credibility, mastering the interpersonal subtleties, fostering the spirit of innovation, and preserving the freedom of expression. These need to be taken up as personal developmental objectives by young aspirants on their own, even though the process may be greatly helped if they are provided with or able to secure mentors who can help in mastering the ten essentials. These ten essentials for evolving as a CEO, presented as a model in Figure 14.2, are outlined below.

Figure 14.2: The Ten Essentials to Become a CEO

1. ***Values and Ethics***

   There is a simple dictum that if one does right things in life, the right results will follow. A young executive should voluntarily follow a set of higher-order ethics and values from the beginning of career. One would be well-advised to not only inculcate an organization's published values and ethics but also search for and absorb what other ethical and value parameters are observed by other leading corporations. Many times, walking the talk, which is a litmus test of leadership, gets inculcated from the young age as one gains strength of character through ethical behaviour.

2. ***Trust and Transparency***

   In business dealings as in social relationships, trust and transparency are critical. A young executive must learn to align his or her thought, expression, and action in a trustworthy and transparent manner. Hidden agendas destroy trust and transparency in organizational relationships. An executive who is known for his transparency is invariably trusted with more responsibilities and partnerships. Trust and transparency arise from a conviction of doing the right things and a confidence of delivering performance against promises made.

3. ***Product-Market Appreciation***

   While behaviours and values are important, alignment with organizational business goals is equally important. As business grows on products and markets, youngsters need to achieve a complete understanding of products and markets, not merely by names but also by characteristics. Understanding the product-market scope is not a responsibility only of sales and marketing personnel; rather it is a requirement for every professional employee. A young executive who fails to grasp the product-market scope early on in his career would never be aligned with the broader organizational value chain.

4. ***Product-Manufacturing Knowledge***

   In an organization, if products constitute the engine of growth, the shopfloor is the platform where manufacturing value is created. The early months of joining an organization is the right period for a young executive to learn the specifications of products and parameters of manufacturing processes. Early integration of value engineering in professional philosophy vests in the young executive an ability to participate in the value creation activities of the organization with greater authenticity, be in products or processes.

5. **Time Management**

   Youngsters, transiting to the generally regulated industry from the relatively flexible academic environment must realize the importance of time, both in personal and business contexts. Time management helps an executive not only to be productive in business but also establish an optimal work–life balance, customized to one's needs. In business, go-to-market time or project launch time is critical, with each participant in the value chain complying with timelines to ensure timely end-delivery. A young executive's appreciation of the importance of time management in business or industry would help him become an astute manager of time in his personal and social life as well.

6. ***Continuous Improvement***

   Integrating a culture of continuous improvement (kaizen) is an essential part of a young executive's career journey. Raising the bar of competitiveness through higher performance on a continuous basis is the way of growth for organizations. A young executive's opportunity and challenge in career lie in his ability to constantly improve. The aspirational young executive typically refuses to accept the status quo and tries to discover ways of doing things better. A spirit of continuous enquiry needs to be the essence of an aspirant's career journey.

7. ***Credibility through Performance***

   A willingness to set stretch targets and a capability to fulfil the promise through performance lends credibility to a young executive's profile. While a policy of "under-promise and over-deliver" is an accepted strategy, true credibility comes with setting challenging targets voluntarily and exceeding them consistently. Such an approach adds great credibility to a young executive's profile. This stems from an ability to conceptualize and analyse the task at hand, estimate elemental times and resource requirements, and successfully execute. A successful chief executive would be one who has been, and is, a thorough project manager.

8. ***Collaborative Networking***

   A young executive needs all the guidance and support from his colleagues and superiors to learn and execute. Unfortunately, human dynamics often destabilize organizational relationships, more so when organizational design and management processes encourage silos. A young executive must treat each colleague as a collaborator and demonstrate how they could be good collaborators. Gaining acceptance of colleagues, treating each one as an internal customer, needs interpersonal skills that in turn require an understanding of human motivation, organizational behaviour, and more importantly an understanding of one's own self.

9. ***Innovative Spirit***

   As one progresses in business or industrial life, competition for leadership tends to be fierce and generic. What differentiates one aspirant of the chief executive position from the other would be the degree of innovation one brings to the job. A young executive who is innovative in his endeavours carves out a niche for himself in the organization. The stamp of innovation could be seen in product creativity, manufacturing efficiency, operational excellence, or business effectiveness. Aspirants of career growth must focus on being innovative in whatever job one does, enhancing organizational competitiveness in the process.

10. ***Freedom of Thought and Expression***

    Most important in a career journey is the ability of an executive to be independent in thinking and execution, within the boundaries and responsibilities set in an organizational system. Freedom of expression must be the cherished trait of an executive as he or she progresses in the organizational journey. The ability to be independent and expressive arises from a sense of rectitude and diligence. Imbibing and demonstrating such ethical behaviour, one also acquires the stature to express the pros and cons fearlessly and take the organization on a competitively and ethically correct path.

Bonsai Managers and Banyan Leaders

Given the pyramid organizational structures, not all young executives can become chief executives in their home organizations, but most young executives can become operational and business leaders of substance and stature in native or other organizations through a combination of behavioural initiatives, knowledge endeavours, and execution efforts. Executives and organizations must collaborate to create organizational ecosystems that facilitate the development of grassroots leadership than a crop of “bonsai managers” and “banyan leaders”—a topic discussed in my book “Leadership for India Inc.”

Chapter 15

Emotional Energy

Emotions are strong feelings that people have. Emotions can be positive as well as negative. Typical emotions, positive and negative, are happiness and sadness, liking and disliking, calmness and anger, politeness and bluntness, confidence and fear, friendship and enmity, trust and mistrust, kindness and jealousy, gentleness and aggression, love and hatred, and so on. Given that organizations are nothing but groups of people, it is but natural that emotions are a part of a typical workplace. The emotional profile of a manager or a leader is a dominant characteristic of a manager or a leader. His or her management and leadership styles become a visible and consistently felt experience for the larger organization. There is often a misplaced view that in organizations negative emotions must necessarily be eliminated and positive emotions mandatorily embedded at the workplace. This is a simplistic view of how business processes and organizational behaviours work.

There have been several theories of emotions from the centuries' prior days of Aristotle to the contemporary days of Stephen Covey, highlighting the need to understand human emotions and for achieving mastery over emotions. In fact, the phrases "emotional balance," "emotional quotient," and "emotional intelligence" have spawned several journal articles and management books on how executives could achieve mastery over their emotions to be effective at the workplace. Important as these are, there is a need to view emotional management at the workplace in terms of intelligent business process management rather than only as an introverted framework of behavioural correction. Fundamental to the concern on the management of emotions is the fact that emotions could affect rational thinking and actions. The paradox of human emotions is rendered more complex when organizations are expected to be embodiments of logical and rational approaches in the conduct of their businesses on one hand, while being driven by hues of emotion such as aggression and passion in achieving superior performance on the other.

Contextual

For most part, emotions need contexts to express themselves. The contextual basis of emotions is that the gap between expectations and accomplishments sets the tone for emotions. If the leader is a stickler for perfection, a perfect process or a perfect outcome from his subordinate makes him or her happy while a shoddy process and outcome makes the leader angry. In the same interaction, if the subordinate knows what perfection is, he or she would display confidence or fear while presenting the process or product. From the simple example that has been considered, emotions emerge from the gaps that exist between expectations and outcomes. The other contextual part of emotions is that people come into organizations as bundles of emotions themselves. In addition, people tend to be of different personality types that will invariably influence how people emote at the workplace. Many employees also do not adequately understand the nexus between their individual roles and performance and the corporate goals and outcomes and anticipate rewards independent of performance. The alignment or gap between career objectives and career growth also leads to emotional dynamics.

Emotions are sharpened by the way they are expressed. The culture of expression, if it is positive, enhances the helpful impact of positive emotions and moderates the erosive impact of negative emotions. The culture of expression, if negative, achieves exactly the opposite. The expressions of verbal language, positive or negative, are further accentuated positively or attenuated negatively by the body language, positive or negative. The part that communication plays in moderating or amplifying emotions is not well understood. Effective and controlled communication is part of emotional balance in organizations. Emotions are not necessarily correlated to circumstances. Crisis situations, contrary to perceptions of chaos, helplessness, and stress, may bring out positive emotions of sharing and caring and of strength and stability amongst the team members. On the other hand, luxurious outcomes may bring out negative emotions of envy and jealousy and of mistrust and aggression among them. The paradox of the contextual perspectives is that emotions are impacted by several internal and external contexts. Figure 15.1 lists a few positive and negative human emotions that impact organizational culture.

Positive Emotions	**Negative Emotions**
Happiness	Anger
Gratitude	Annoyance
Peacefulness	Sadness
Hope	Guilt
Inspiration	Fear
Altruism	Anxiety
Satisfaction	Despair
Affection	Apathy
Admiration	Frustration
Enthusiasm	Depression

Figure 15.1: Human Emotions Impact Organizational Culture

It is also incorrect to assume that positive emotions are always beneficial and negative ones detrimental. If team members are not mature enough and instead are subservient to emotions in appraising performance, performance management would be at a discount. In such cases where the employees and their supervisors lack the ability to differentiate task delivery from emotional wrapping, people may be classified into emotional archetypes. Emotions, whether positive or negative, are likely to introduce skew, bias, and halo effects in relationships if emotions are not objectively and discriminatingly expressed or understood. Emotional balancing may help the groups manage positive or negative performance in a stable manner only if emotional expression is indexed to the context of task delivery of individuals, teams, and organizations.

If managers and teams as well as cross-functional peers ensure clear target setting with joint ownership, and alignment on objectives, resources and evaluation criteria, the chances for emotional upheavals, positive or negative, would be minimized. Another hypothesis could be that the industry context would determine the emotional texture of an organization. Market- and customer-facing organizations may be postulated to be more emotionally sensitive compared to manufacturing organizations. Domains like advertising and consumer research may be more emotionally interactive than others. In practice, however, emotional sensitivity and responsiveness are related more to gaps between expectations, accomplishments, communications competency levels, independent of any domain or industry. The movie industry whose organizations and team members are characterised by emotive artistic elements in all its aspects, for example, has all the interpersonal emotional fallibilities as any other industrial organization; if at all, the movie industry has an even greater level of emotional dynamics.

Tolerances and Controls

As in engineering design, the theory of tolerances plays a vital role in emotional management too. People, in the organizational context, must observe tolerances in mutual expression of emotions. While not all emotions may be appropriate in an organizational context, a few have relevance. While a gentle, trusting, caring, sharing, and joyous emotional outlook may enhance positive energy in a team, excessive levels of such positive emotions could be counterproductive. While fun at work is desirable, it cannot be only fun at work to the detriment of stretch and challenge at work. At the same time, an aggressive, evaluative, demanding, consolidating, and sombre emotional outlook may bring out the right amount of fear and adrenal rush in the face of adversity or complacence. While fear is the key to compliance and achievement, fearful authoritarianism cannot be endorsed to the detriment of creativity and innovation at work. Clearly, only if teams can play upon their positive and negative emotions within fine tolerances that are synergistic in the organizational context, emotions can be helpful.

This chapter proposes the concept of Intelligent Emotional Balance (IEB) to optimize the emotional energy in an organization. At the core of IEB lies the ability to understand the emotional sensitivity of self and others and develop the ability to control the emergence and expression of emotions in an organizationally appropriate manner. This approach does not mean that people should or would lose their spontaneity. It merely recognizes that an organization has certain primary performance metrics to deliver on a day-today basis. A culture of emotional sensitivity, in fact, helps the team modulate performance expectation and delivery achievements. The model of IEB has three vital components: the first, understanding the importance of a person's own and his team members' emotional proclivities; the second, an understanding of the tolerances within which mutual emotions become synergistic rather than antagonistic; and the third, a competence to control emotions to be supportive of a virtuous organizational culture. An ability to retain rationality, objectivity, and logic in the face of exciting opportunities and depressing setbacks alike with just the right touch of humanism helps spread the positive vibrations of energy across the organization. Figure 15.2 presents the intelligent emotional balance model.

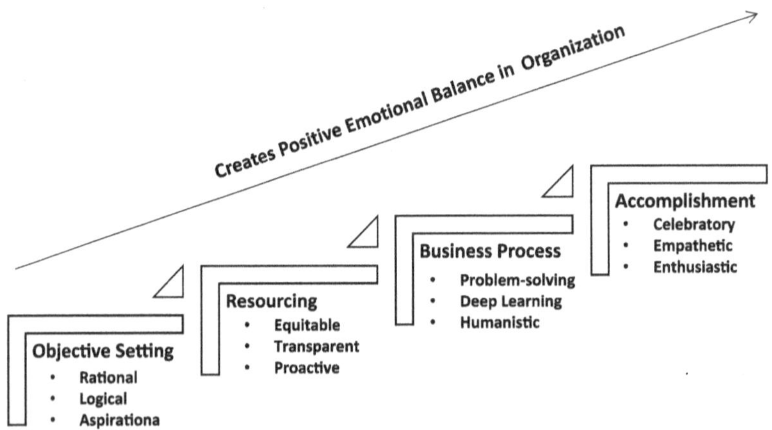

Figure 15.2: Intelligent Emotional Balance Model

IEB Model in Practice

An organization can achieve IEB when its leaders practise the optimal business processes that enable a sense of fulfilment in day-to-day work, thereby enabling appropriate emotional balance. The optimum business process does not end merely with objective setting or questioning but incorporates problem solving where required. A leader who sets a challenging technical task for his subordinate logically expects the subordinate to deliver, failing which finds it rational to take the subordinate to task. The IEB model, in this case, expects that the leader does not merely stop at expressing his unhappiness but also empathizes with the subordinate's incapacity to deliver and sets about to work with the subordinate to develop a solution. Once the subordinate develops the solution to the leader's satisfaction, the leader joyously celebrates with the subordinate, thus wiping clean the earlier unhappiness and opening a new chapter of collaboration. In another case where the subordinate succeeds in terms of delivery, the leader celebrates with the subordinate first but goes on to prescribe a higher level of challenge for the subordinate that leads the organization onto a path of continuous achievement and fulfilment.

A purely emotional view of achievement leads to a sense of complacence and distances the participants from the competitive scenario that exists in the outside business world. Setting expectations appropriately, reinforcing competencies commensurately, providing resources adequately, evaluating results objectively, coaching for improved results empathetically, learning from failures confidently, and celebrating successes with humility provide an optimal IEB in an organization. The leaders and managers can help facilitate the institution of IEB by being themselves role models of the following: (i) equidistance from, or equal attachment to, functions and people, (ii) adaptive of rational and emotionally balanced business and communication processes, (iii) focused on competency development and task delivery, (iv) controlled and balanced in experiencing and expressing emotions, (v) learning openly from setbacks and failures, and (vi) optimally celebrating successes with humility. The foregoing leadership model would help institutionalize the broader IEB model on a sustainable basis in the organization.

Chapter 16

Traits and Behaviour

"We value our people" is the almost universal averment of all progressive corporations. To give the benefit of doubt, corporations and leaders who espouse this corporate value are sincere to the statement. In day-to-day recruitment, performance management, and talent development, however, there tends to be an incredible emphasis on recruiting good candidates, rewarding good performance, and helping employees become better, respectively. Several behavioural tools are adopted to enable individuals better understand themselves and contribute to their improved individual performance and logically therefore better corporate performance. Firms also go to significant lengths to define the desirable characteristics in the context of the business the firms operate in. Over the years, the concept of team as being the overarching concept took root but the emphasis on individual has not faded, rightly so. Over the years, businesses have become more complex with competition for scarce resources and yearning for extraordinary growth.

Businesses have also become more globally networked with pressures for multicultural outlook and compulsions for global competitiveness. Disruptive digital technologies are transforming industries and impacting individual firms. The traits one looks for success in, and through, individuals have become a legion, making one wonder whether organizations have started looking for super-humans as managers and leaders, if not as employees. If the company has clearly articulated goals, robust strategies and plans to work to, and a relentless focus on execution, all with clearly defined structures and processes, even ordinary individuals and teams would deliver. Several models, as discussed in my book "Leadership for India Inc." can be adopted to drive team and individual performance at a firm level. This chapter proposes that all these expectations and models work only if the Big Five personality traits as discussed herein are recognized and encouraged at the firm level.

Exciting Diversity

Life is made more interesting by the variability in human behaviour. If everyone were to think and act exactly like each other, life would be robotic. As we cruise through our schools, colleges, and organizations, we can perceive, see, feel, and appreciate substantial differences among our friends and colleagues. Such variability introduces a rich diversity of culture and lifestyle into the society. A principal reason why a foreign national, or even an Indian, is both flummoxed and excited about India is the rich cultural tapestry across its states and the varied behavioural nuances amongst individuals of different regions. It is sobering to think that no amount of education or indoctrination can morph the behavioural approaches of a varied population. This, for example, is as natural as a Japanese not thinking or acting like an American, and vice versa. Yet, successful business gets done between culturally differentiated nations.

That said, when organizations are established with specific objectives of focused performance for shared goals, it is necessary that inter-individual differences are kept within certain tolerance levels, much like a product characteristic is measured and reviewed in statistical quality control. Also, the behavioural volatility within an individual must operate within an acceptable amplitude for organizations to work in a harmonious yet exciting manner. All the theories of management, despite their elegant constructs, do not provide an authentic basis for understanding why employees behave as they do. An understanding of the structural basis of inter-individual and within-individual differences in human behaviour and cognition would be necessary. Such an understanding would help organizations and leaders neither dismiss such differences as "noise" nor accept them as "destiny." The concept of tracking and managing diversity and volatility in organizations is pictorially presented in Figure 16.1.

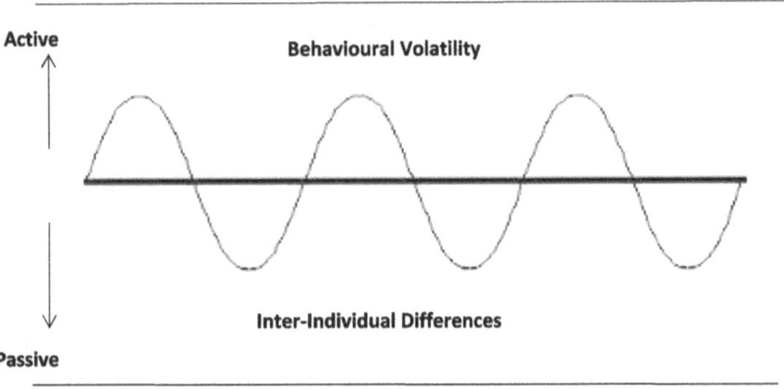

Figure 16.1: Managing Diversity and Volatility in Organizations

Neuroscience

Neuroscience has emerged as an important branch of study that can help identify variability in perception, thought, and action between individuals and within individuals. Methods that provide measures of brain's neural activity (such as fMRI, electroencephalography (EEG), positron emission topography (PET), magnetic resonance spectroscopy (MRS), and diffusion tensor imaging (DTI)) have been used to study the neural bases of individual differences in cognition. Journals dedicated to neuroscience, psychology, and psychiatry routinely carry several scholarly and research-based articles on how such methods can identify the structural basis for interindividual differences. For example, one of the critical parameters of leadership is decision-making capability. In decision-making, fast decisions in most cases come at the risk of reduced accuracy. This phenomenon of speed–accuracy trade-off as well as the switch between cautious and risky behaviours have been studied in neuroscience by performing fMRI studies of certain brain circuitry.

Neuroscience explains why certain individuals would have more specialized skills than others. It even explains why grey matter in a physiological sense is important for determining various cognitive capabilities of different individuals. While neuroscience may offer great clues to explaining human behaviour patterns, it is unlikely to be of any real-time help to corporate leaders in understanding and managing individual and organizational behaviour. MRI scans cannot obviously be the recruitment filters; nor can MRIs be used to select members for collaborative or competitive team formations. Just as psychological assessments of human behaviour have their limitations in assessing managerial potential, even the more diagnostic neuroscience studies may not necessarily help select employees who could possess the desired cognitive capabilities. That said, neuroscience studies may throw light on the personality and intelligence traits that could be of relevance in specific organizational contexts.

Big Five Traits

While there exist over 100 personality traits in management literature, the Big Five Theory of human psychology hypothesizes that five core traits make up human personality. Psychologists use these five traits to describe the fundamental dimensions of personality traits. These comprise four positive traits and one potentially negative trait. The four positive traits are openness, conscientiousness, extroversion, and agreeableness while the negative trait is neuroticism, together referred by the acronym OCEAN. Research has shown that each of the traits correlates with certain anatomical dispositions of different regions of the brain. Psychometric questionnaire inventory seeks to quantify the level of each of the fundamental dimensions and more recent research is attempting to establish a correlation between the results of questionnaires and the results of brain imaging studies. In future, face recognition technologies and body sensor technologies together with artificial intelligence may help find the right talent.

While such developments are welcome, the enormity of the task in relation to multitudes of international cultures and millions of individuals makes universal applicability a practical impossibility. It behoves organizational experts to define the factors in organizational context, and help employees appreciate their traits in terms of individual amplitude and interindividual diversity with a view to harmonize for realizing individual and organizational effectiveness. Extroversion (or extraversion) is the trait of being lively and confident and possessing the quality of enjoying being with other people. It is characterized by sociability and talkativeness as well as assertiveness and excitability. Extroversion is seen as a key leadership enabler. Conscientiousness is the quality of taking care to be able to do things carefully and correctly. It reflects dutifulness and self-discipline. Openness is the quality of being honest and not hiding information or feelings. It is also about the quality of being able to listen to, think about, and accept other people and other ideas. Agreeableness is the quality of being pleasant and easy to like. It reflects a tendency to be empathetic and cooperative. Neuroticism is a core trait with shades of negativity like being worried and being prone to experience and express unpleasant emotions easily (like anger, anxiety, depression, and vulnerability). If an employee needs to be successful, the four positive traits of emotional stability and affinity must be strongly displayed, and the negative trait of emotional instability must be minimized. Figure 16.2 presents the Big Five personality trait model.

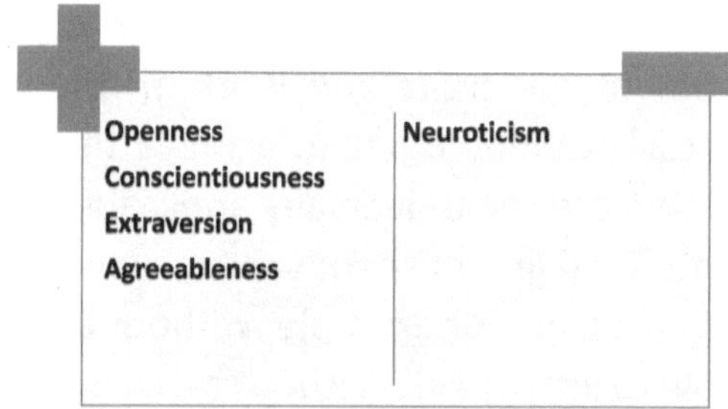

Figure 16.2: The Big Five Personality Traits Model

Big Five Challenge

The task of maintaining a beneficial balance between the positive four traits and the negative one trait together is challenging because life is so stressful and competitive that constantly the positive traits are suppressed, and the negative trait is stoked by people, events, and processes. As the rewards and recognition systems in organizations are governed, by and large, by the final outcomes with little to differentiate on which traits worked for which winners, the tendency is to adopt the personality traits that provide winning outcomes overall. With the proliferation of "trait theories," there is also a greater emphasis on visible and surrogate traits rather than the fundamental traits. It is important that conscious and persistent efforts are made by individuals and their stakeholders (be they parents, friends, or teachers) to instil (or enable the ability to enhance) the positive traits and minimize (or instil the ability to moderate) the negative trait. As one's consciousness increases with age and education, focus should be laid on the importance of the Big Five traits.

The biological origins of the basic personality traits cannot be ignored. Research has shown how the grey matter in various segments of the brain correlates with the level of each of the five fundamental traits. This, however, tends to be a biological uniqueness for an individual. What one can do, however, is to be cognizant of the traits and work on them. Literature suggests several methodologies to achieve this. Observation and introspection are the universally applicable methods that are simple yet effective. These, however, require some of the basic traits themselves. For example, without being open, one may not be able to introspect. Without being an extrovert, one may not have a team to interact and observe at all. If a person is not agreeable, one may not receive feedback at all from such a person. Similarly, if one is neurotic, one would miss the perspectives of objectivity and analysis. The importance of constantly working on the five core traits in life's progression is self-evident.

Ancient Indian Science

To circle back to where we started, organizations do value people. However, it is to be understood that people are valued, in a true sense, for the positive traits they display and stand for. All outstanding leaders are epitomes of positive traits (besides, of course, technical, scientific, or professional competencies that are called for). While an individual is, by and large, responsible for his or her own development, organizations can gain greatly by creating ecosystems that promote positive traits in employees. What the typical organization seeks by way of competitiveness can be achieved only when it has employees who are open, conscientious, extraverted, and agreeable, and nonneurotic. This chapter demonstrates that rather than become diffused over multiple traits, it would be sensible for individuals and organizations to focus on these five core traits to reflect upon and develop.

While modern science has provided imaging and neuroscience as two potent aids to understand individual traits and intra- as well as inter-individual differences in traits, these aspects are still research works in process; they are also too expensive and too impractical to be of use on a routine basis. Fortunately, ancient Indian science has provided a much simpler and more universally deployable methodology to develop one's traits positively. Yoga and meditation are ancient Indian sciences that can be of help in shaping the Big Five traits with positive bias. Enlightened organizations have, therefore, started giving importance to yoga and meditation. Many high-level leadership programs incorporate, these days, sessions on yoga, meditation, and spirituality by respected gurus such as Swami Sukhabodhananda, Sri Sri Ravishankar and Jaggi Vasudev, who are well known for their coaching on value-based leadership.

Chapter 17

Perception Dynamics

Life is a game of chance between perception and reality. Nature is reality but human nature is largely one of perception. Human beings struggle to discover the "real" you or me, in the process, viewing perceptions as the realities. Reality is the true situation that exists in life while perception is the way one notices the true situation in life. The enlightened or the "jnani," as defined in a Hindu philosophical sense, perceives reality as the reality and is open in bringing out the real person. Given that most individuals fail to reach or do not wish to reach the state of enlightenment, perceptions are also different from realities. The conflict and contrast between the reality and perception underpins the challenges of day-to-day human dynamics and influences the course of organizational behaviour. It is appropriate to, therefore, understand the implications of the reality–perception paradigm.

The discourse on perception and reality is carried out in two schools. One school holds that it is irrelevant to seek to discover what the reality is when an individual is a social and economic being, conditioned by several benchmarks and aspirations. This school maintains that in any organization, be it the family, educational institution, or the employer, individuals are bound by certain common goals, the fulfilment of which is the responsibility and obligation of individuals, independent of their own and their organizational realities. The other school believes that all human discontent and strife is due to the mismatch between reality and perception, both about oneself and the others. This school maintains that if only people understand the realities completely, there would be greater equity and equanimity in human dynamics. Figure 17.1 pictorially depicts conditioners and enablers that will be discussed in the forthcoming subsections.

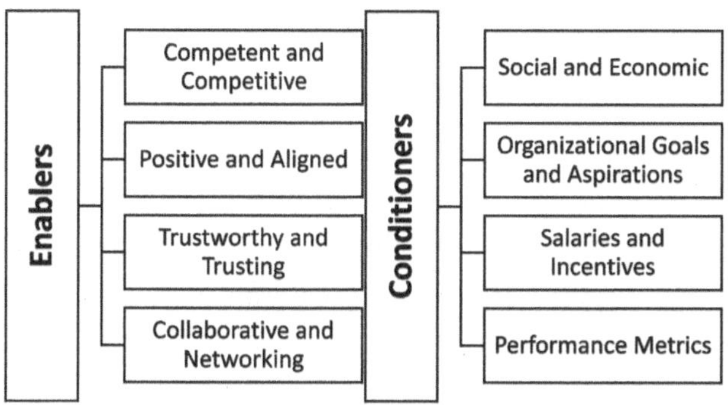

Figure 17.1: Conditioners and Enablers

Conditioners

Human life, though a creation of nature, is not a natural life; it is a conditioned life. Social and economic conditioners modify behaviour patterns consciously or subconsciously such that external perceptions are different from internal realities. They also blur the ability of individuals to at least note, if not analyse and improve upon, the realities. From an individual perspective, family and friends are the most significant conditioners that define one's values, attitudes, aspirations, and performance metrics. As a result, often individuals exist and live for the goals and aspirations set by the conditioners rather than those set by their heart and mind. That said, it is neither wrong nor right to lead a conditioned life that looks after others' interests rather than one's own. If such living does not lead to major conflicts between perception and reality, such conditioned life could be socially and economically fulfilling.

To achieve that, individuals need to introspect for reality and adjust for perceptions. Organizational life, a creation of human beings, on the other hand, is explicitly designed to fulfil the needs of the society and the economy. It is conditioned to perpetually grow. It does not matter if the team members are diverse in their educational and experience backgrounds and heterogeneous in their social and economic conditioning. Their objective is to fulfil organizational goals of serving the society and economy with appropriate products and services. Unlike in a purely individual life, a corporation must look after its interests by primarily serving the needs of the consumers. The individuals of an organization, ipso facto, must serve the broader organizational goals. For that to happen, all organizational members must function harmoniously. Many times, organizations believe that salaries and incentives are the conditioners for such performance. However, the triggers are different.

Enablers

Organizations would be successful when they collaborate internally and compete externally. A successful organization would require each of its team members to be competitive in his or her trade, but the organization cannot afford to have team members who compete, mistrust or confront internally. For team members to be internally collaborative, communication is the key. For communication between people to be effective, trust is essential. Trust develops when people are perceived to be open and collaborative. The closed loop of collaboration illustrates that perceptions of collaborative behaviour are essential to ensure a reality of internal collaboration. For an organization to be an effective competitor, it is essential to have internal collaboration amongst the various functions and individuals of an organization. Companies that practice concurrent engineering and coordinated delivery, for example, are more successful than those that are prone to sequential, or stage gated development and delivery. Perceptions are the key enablers of collaboration.

People constantly make judgments of each other's behaviour while they also tend to straitjacket themselves into certain behaviour patterns. These patterns range from affable to aggressive, and consensual to assertive, for example. In addition, people are often perceived in terms of both positive perceptions (for example, helpful, selfless, knowledgeable, and empathetic) and negative perceptions (for example, unhelpful, selfish, pedestrian, and arrogant). It is important for individuals and team managers to identify and reinforce contextually relevant positive traits and eliminate contextually counterproductive negative traits. The organizational challenge is two-fold; first, select people who have real attributes that are as close as possible to the desired organizational benchmarks and second, develop people so that their perceived behaviours are aligned to the desired organizational benchmarks.

Perception Grid

Like all management challenges, perception management requires a conceptual and analytical framework. The 2×2 perception grid, which this chapter proposes, enables such conceptualization and analysis. The grid has on the X-axis positive and negative perceptions, and on the Y-axis enablers and disablers. The four subgrades that are possible are enablers of positive perceptions (EPP), enablers of negative perceptions (ENP), disablers of positive perceptions (DPP), and disablers of negative perceptions (DNP). Clearly, an organizational ecosystem that maximizes the EPP and DNP grids and minimizes the DPP and ENP grids is an ideal goal. This goal is easier set than achieved, however. There are two major reasons for a preponderance of the suboptimal organizational ecosystems. Firstly, people embed and exhibit certain time-ossified personality types. Secondly, different organizational situations require different personality dispositions and individuals; besides, managers may lack maturity and flexibility to adapt and change. Figure 17.2 demonstrates the perception grid that connects positive and negative perceptions with enablement and disablement.

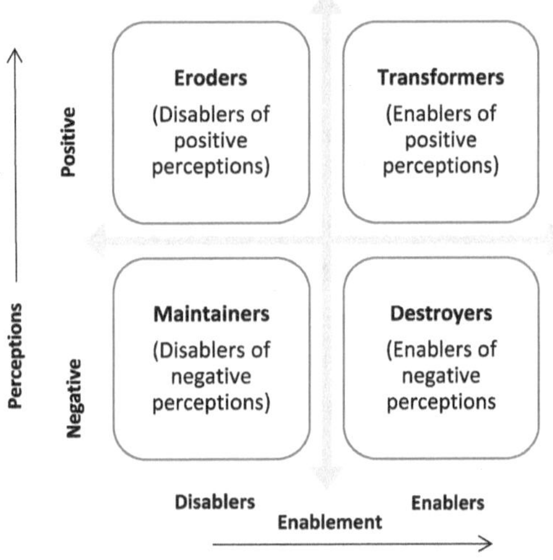

Figure 17.2: Perception Grid

Positive perceptions of a person essentially arise from one's knowledge, how productively one deploys it, and how positively one communicates it. The level of positivity tends to be adversely impacted if any of the three factors of knowledge, deployment, and communication is compromised. Negative perceptions of a person essentially arise from lack of knowledge, inability to apply available knowledge, and a resistant approach to disseminate knowledge. The level of negativity tends to be further worsened if any of the three factors is deficient. In both the cases, communication plays a major part. People in the EPP and DNP grids are likely to be highly positive communicators, whereas individuals in the ENP and DPP grids are likely to be negative communicators. The three determinants of communication are content, style, and empathy. The positivity of communication is enhanced by the strength of content, the coherence of delivery, and the trust created by empathy. The pathway to a collaborative team lies in reinforcing positive perceptions through the three positive traits and enabling positive communication through the three components.

Perceptive Ability

Perception is a state that is different from reality but imagined to be the reality. Perceptive ability denotes an ability to see or understand things quickly and correctly, especially things that are not obvious. An individual must have a perceptive ability to understand how one is perceived. While ideally, the real and perceived personality must be the same, it may not always be so. Perception could be different from the reality. The real persona, under certain circumstances, must be subordinate to the desired perception that is set in the team context. In business negotiations, for example, perceptions of aggressive behaviour do no good to the process. In the field of teaching and public speaking, introverts tend to don the mantle of extroverts to fulfil their responsibility.

Individuals who stray off their careers of aptitude reshape themselves to match up to their accountabilities and responsibilities in such different careers. While one need not be either artificial or affected, one must understand how one must carry oneself gracefully and in a positively influential manner, based on the strategic context. A virtuous organization would comprise individuals who have positive traits and who promote positivity in relationships. The organization would be knowledge-based, task-focused, performance-driven, relationship-oriented, communication-savvy, and apolitical. The leaders would be evangelists rather than enforcers, and mentors rather than managers. The individual team members, rather than analysing themselves and others in a quest for difficult-to-discover realties, would endeavour to develop and appreciate positive perceptions. This is not to suggest that a collaborative organization is based only on positive perceptions and positive communication. As discussed earlier, one must be positively real in terms of knowledge, its deployment, and its dissemination as well as in terms of content, style, and empathy of communication. There can be no reality compromise on these six critical factors of positive perception.

Chapter 18

Networking for Success

Relationship is at the core of social evolution. Relationship is the way in which two or more people or things relate to each other. While relationships are usually interpreted in terms of family ties and friendly moorings, relationships extend far beyond family cocoons or friendship circles. In a broader perspective, relationship is the way in which two or more people or groups regard and behave towards each other. Many such relationships that are beyond the family system are experienced by us; for example, the teacher–student relationship, the doctor–patient relationship, the employer–employee relationship, the property owner–tenant relationship, the people–government relationship, the buyer–seller relationship, the multiple stakeholder relationships, and so on.

In fact, virtually everyone has a relationship with someone else he or she deals with, in one way or the other. At the very basic level, the awareness of one another results in just a cognitive relationship. As it evolves into an acquaintance, a reciprocating relationship develops. Reciprocation could just be in the form of exchange of greetings or could extend to exchange of information or other material factors. While one could experience hundreds of reciprocal relationships, only a few would evolve into sustainable relationships. For a relationship to be sustainable, the relationship must traverse through three stages. The first is rapport, the second is credibility, and the third is trust. Rapport exists when two people or agencies have a close and harmonious relationship, understanding each other's feelings and ideas, and communicating well. Credibility exists when one stands convincing, believable and, capable of fulfilling the promise, in a consistent manner. Repeated demonstration of credibility leads to a firm belief in the truth, reliability, and ability of someone or something. Trust has, in most cases, a material fiduciary responsibility and accountability. Figure 18.1 illustrates the three phases of relationship.

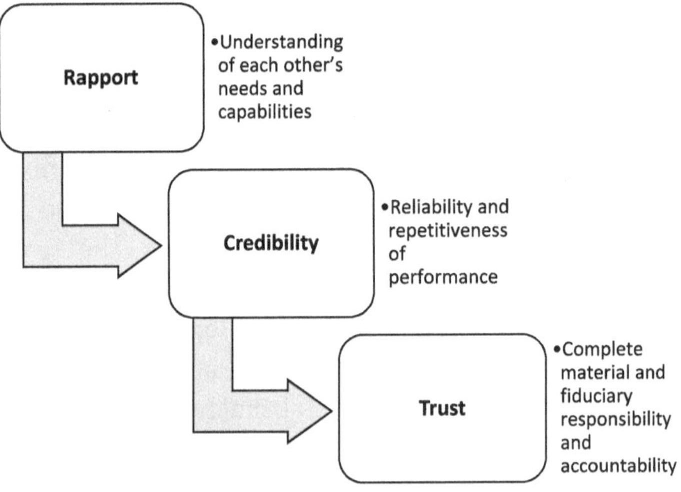

Figure 18.1: The Three Phases of Relationship

Business Relationships

Business relations are varied; from one-off casual interactions to legally binding business contracts, there are many ways in which business relations evolve. Some relationships are business to business (B2B), whereas some are business to consumer (B2C). There are others like business to government, which are legal and regulatory, and certain others such as business to society, which are more qualitative and abstract. Whatever be the nature of relationship, the three-step process defined above, and comprising "rapport, credibility, and trust" is necessary.

Even in the case of one-off transactional relationships, the process builds value for the present or for the future. Business managements have traditionally seen financial ownership and/or commercial partnership, with legal structuring, as the predominant basis to form and protect relationships, but there is more to it. Relationships are also subject to competitive dynamics. Exclusive dealerships have, in the past, been the preferred relationships for sales and marketing. Over a period, multi-brand dealerships have started appearing (whether in the same dealer format or co-owned dealer format). Simultaneously, companies started setting up selling plazas dedicated to different product groups (for example, Maruti Nexa for higher end cars). Just as social relationships are influenced by the dynamics of families and friends, business relations are also influenced by competitive dynamics. Any amount of legal mandating may not help when competitive dynamics disturb. These influences could be for cost and price advantages or growth compulsions. These could also be due to lack of relationship between the people who manage the relationships.

Interpersonal Complexities

Business relationships are far more complex than usually imagined. Business Relationship Management is not as simple as measuring performance or profits as generally thought to be. Each business relation is, in fact, a complex maze of interpersonal relationships. There are three such principal complexities.

The first is generational complexity. When first set up, later managed, or eventually terminated, it is people who interpret and endorse or negate a business relationship. A business relationship has four distinct phases: commercial discovery, legal templating, operational performance, and performance review. All the phases are carried out by individuals on either side of the relationship. As individuals change, not only the dynamics change but the initial perspectives tend to be lost.

The second is horizontal complexity. Although a transaction is fulfilled at one end of a business value chain, the actual utility could be far out in the value chain. A typical example is a vendor relationship that could impact manufacturing, and thereafter customer delivery. If persons leading or operating at different points of the value chain cannot communicate holistically and meaningfully with each other, even simple performance issues could lead to enormous noise in the system and destabilize relationships.

The third is vertical complexity. Certain business relationships are initiated, structured, and signed off at the top between senior leaders, and handed over to operating teams below to execute. While the jobs may be handed down, the perspectives and the subtleties may never be cascaded down. In certain other cases, a business relationship may be established at the operating level but could come to the notice of, and review by, senior leaders at a later stage. The juniors may not be able to explain appropriately, or even lack the strategic approach the senior leadership now takes. This could also create noise in the system. Given that business relationships are built on interpersonal foundations, the need for a systemic yet a people-oriented approach to business relationships is self-evident. Five principles for successful and sustainable business relationships are discussed below.

Five Principles

There are five principles of trustworthy and trusting business relationships that can be built with the interpersonal trust model. Figure 18.2 presents the model of five success factors for sustainable business relationship.

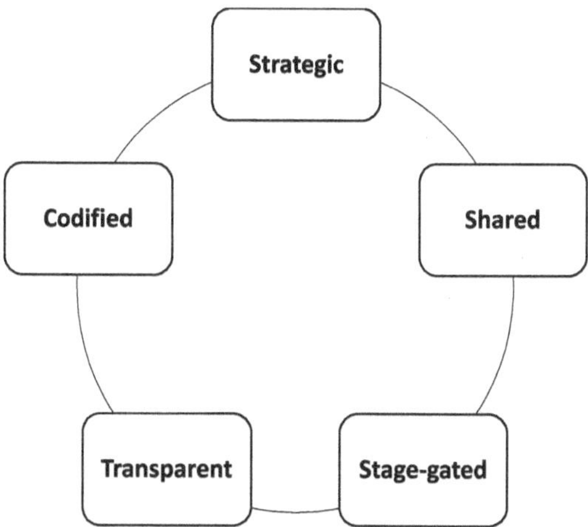

Figure 18.2: Success Factors for Sustainable Business Leadership

1. ***Strategic***

   Not every business relationship is, or needs to be, made at the CEO or CXO levels. Consistent with the nature of a business relationship, the highest leader must, however, be involved. A new green-field expansion by a component supplier needs certainly CEO-to-CEO partnership. However, an arrangement for housekeeping will not require such intervention; yet, within the boundary, at least the functional managers must be involved from either side. The involvement of senior managers and leaders helps in the avoidance of "penny wise and pound foolish" approaches and instead focus on long-term value creation. The involvement of strategic leaders ensures that the operating executives are not threatened by a self-perceived need to save the pennies at the cost of long-term value.

2. ***Risk-Based***

   All relations aim at rewards. It would be fallacious, however, to assume that there are risk-free approaches to business relationships. The more novel a business relationship is, the higher the risk profile could be, even as its competitive advantage could be higher. If the relation follows a beaten or established path, it suffers from another type of risk of eroding margins. No amount of legally binding contractual language can identify and provide for all current and future risks. Interpersonal rapport, credibility, and trust help in addressing risk professionally. One may have a perfectly collaborative relationship with a competitor (like Apple and Samsung have between them) when the risk and reward tracks are not intermixed, and respective leaders are allowed to deal with competitive and collaborative aspects separately.

3. ***Stage-Gated***

   Business relationships should not be founded on expectations of immediate miraculous results. Adequate time should be allowed for operational teams to strike rapport, prove credibility, and establish trust. Leaders have a particular responsibility in selecting lead managers who have positive interpersonal approaches and sound fundamentals. Many times, conceptually sound partnerships flounder because of cantankerous managers who are self-obsessed rather than focused on mutual value creation. If the first stage of rapport does not take place, the sponsor-leaders have a responsibility to either counsel the lead managers or replace them with more harmonious ones. Similarly, if credibility is not established with repetitive consistent performance, the processes must be relooked. Normally, a quarter of rapport building and another quarter of credibility establishment, at the maximum, may be allowed to assess the precursors to trust. And transparency is the key to assessment of trust.

4. ***Transparent***

   Transparency starts from the initiation of a business relationship. Mature leaders realize that placing mutual expectations, strengths, weaknesses, and resource capabilities on the discussion table help establish the fundamental rules of transparency in a business relationship. Many do not realize that understanding the weaknesses of partners helps build greater strengths in the relationship. For example, when an Indian outsourcing partner does not have global sourcing strength, and discloses that weakness upfront, the sponsoring client would be able to leverage its own global sourcing network to meet the gaps. This transparency may cost the outsourcing partner a pricing advantage, and the sponsoring company an overhead burden but will provide to both greater business value. Transparency helps in win–win alliances as well as in developing trust to handle risks and share rewards equitably.

5. ***Codified***

   There are two ways to handle interpersonal complexities, whether generational, horizontal, or vertical. One way is to have the same people handle the business relation, longitudinally in time, horizontally in value chain, and vertically in hierarchy. In this case, institutionalized knowledge and practice keeps building on established relationships. However, "people-perpetuity" is hardly possible, and not desirable too either. People must be moved in and out of positions, and careers; and even if they stay static, changes in business environments with new competitive dynamics induce changes in people. The only insulation can be through the codification of perspectives, processes, and expectations with which a relationship is set up, and the implicit and explicit value from the relationship. Partnership codification must be a living document, enriched with progressive setbacks and accomplishments.

Partnership as Relationship

Partnership, in a legal meaning, is an association between persons or entities that involves the pooling of all resources and sharing of all assets and liabilities, usually in the ratio in which respective resources are brought in by the parties. Partnership, in practice, is the consummate form of a relationship that brings in the concepts of sharing equally and equitably. Relationship is a generic way of two entities connecting with each other, whereas partnership is a customized definition of an equitable relationship. Partnership signifies a shared future. There are times when partnership itself must reflect an even more sublime relationship.

Partnerships are challenged when one of the partners is beset by serious business troubles for extended periods of time. Imagine the relationship between a truck maker who makes only trucks and is hit by recession and a component maker who caters to all types of automobiles, some of them growing in demand. If the component maker agrees to price reductions to support the truck maker and stays on through the cycle of recession collaboratively without shifting capacity, it goes beyond partnership; it will be companionship. Similar is the case of a multi-brand retailer who is willing to retain shelf space and digital space for a fading product company engaged in reinventing its products. Strange it may seem in a hardnosed business context, companionship is the sublime form of business relationship, as in personal relationships.

Chapter 19

Later as the Latest

Many times, in life, we are so obsessed with symptoms that we lose sight of the root cause. Also, many times we mistake a part to be the whole. True, management thought has taught us to focus on results. True also that the industrial engineering movement, and even the famed Toyota Production System, taught us the benefits of division of work and specialization. In general, if each person does what he or she is supposed to do right, the next in sequence would occur with equal efficiency. Efficient parts, it is believed, make for an effective whole. This indeed is logical but only as long as the logic of what must override what in terms of the core purpose is appreciated.

The issue at hand is almost like the distinction between Ayurveda, the ancient Indian science of healing and Allopathy, the modern practice of medicine. The former requires a patient to be studied in whole before a disease is treated. The Ayurvedic treatments offered in India are a case in point. Allopathy believes that unless the disease as expressed by the symptoms is addressed quickly, there could be collateral damage. Obviously, both approaches have their merits and applicability. The debate, however, makes us think through what is primary and what is secondary in the real sense, and reprise the meanings of the various practices we are accustomed to in life. Some interesting examples, relevant for individuals, managers, leaders, and organizations alike, follow.

Dilemmas of Learning

Learning is a lifelong experience. Most of the learning is focused on developing for oneself an organized set of knowledge which can be deployed by individuals in their life avocations. Schools, colleges, institutes, and universities are the organizations that are at hand for this activity of knowledge acquisition. Figure 19.1 summarizes the dilemmas of learning. These are discussed below briefly.

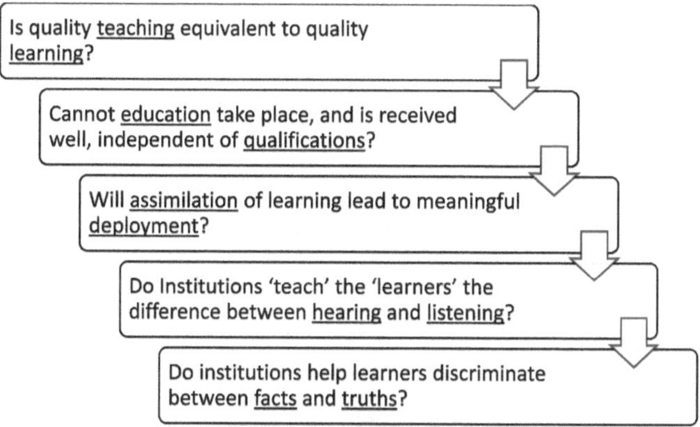

Figure 19.1: The Dilemmas of Learning

1. ***Teaching and Learning***

   There is much focus on institutes that offer quality teaching. This focus is not peculiar to India; it pervades even the advanced countries. The basic purpose, one would presume, of good teaching is good learning. One should logically look for institutes that enable good learning rather than that offer good teaching. Good teaching need not necessarily translate itself into good learning. In any case, rather than assume that good teaching makes students good learners, it would be appropriate to insist on teachers as well as students to focus on learning. While assessing graduates of institutes, it is important to assess if they had assimilated learning to the standard equivalent to the teaching that the institute is expected to provide.

2. ***Qualifications and Education***

   As with the chase for quality teaching institutes, there is an equal, if not greater, craze for educational qualifications and professional certifications. Without doubt, formal qualifications are essential means of ensuring that one goes through a prescribed process of education and evaluation. However, education can take place independent of qualifications, and all qualifications may not result in the same level of education. The challenge is greater when people acquire diverse qualifications. Whether one qualification de-educates one of the previous qualifications or builds on the foundations is a key aspect. While assessing individuals with or without qualifications, it is important to assess the true level of education and learning he or she would have got.

3. ***Assimilation and Application***

   The main purpose of teaching and learning is to help a learner assimilate all knowledge within oneself. As modern research indicates, the human brain is an amazing library and storehouse of whatever information is deposited into it. Contrary to popular belief, the brain can absorb an endless array of information. Unlike a physical library, even if information is sought to be taken out from the brain, it remains in the memory; in fact, it becomes expanded depending on the way the retrieved information is processed and acted upon. Assimilation is purposeless without application, just as teaching is purposeless without learning. Application of knowledge is the one that differentiates active achievers from passive followers. It is also interesting that it is the greater application of knowledge rather than just greater teaching or learning that results in greater assimilation of knowledge.

4. ***Hearing and Listening***

   Hearing is the electromechanical process of receiving external sounds through the ears, whether from nature or humans. Every sound has its purpose and meaning, more so the speech of humans. In fact, the productivity of human relationships is based entirely on communication. Communication is complete only when the message is listened to, rather than merely heard. Listening, as contrasted with hearing, is the process of paying attention with a view to hear and/or hearing with an intention to take notice. Listening, therefore, is purposeful hearing. Hearing without listening does not contribute to human bonding.

5. ***Facts and Truths***

   Facts are real incidents that have occurred, but truth is what they represent. The fact of one studying for long hours does not necessarily represent the truth or untruth of studying with concentration. Facts are visible and can be recounted with accuracy. Truth is invisible and can be only inferred or evaluated when disclosed. All truth is not factually discoverable, whereas all facts may not disclose the entire truth. The dilemma in an active and speedy life is to whether to progress on facts as received or become stalled in a potentially endless search for truth.

Dilemmas of Deployment

India has significant educational infrastructure and talent pool. There are many ways by which knowledge can be deployed but the ways in which the deployment can lead to competitiveness are more appropriate. Figure 19.2 summarizes the five key paradoxes of deployment. These are discussed below briefly.

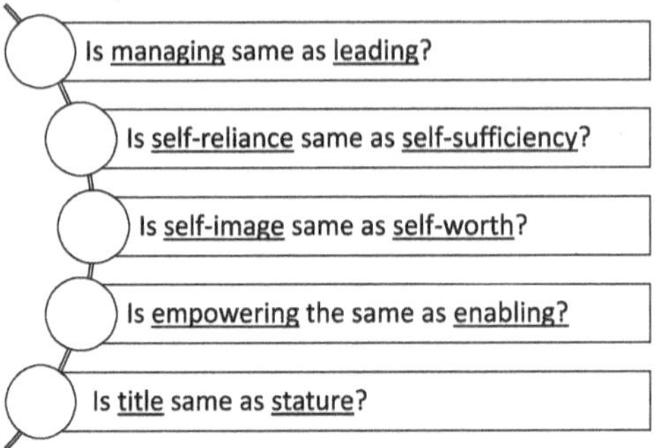

Figure 19.2: The Paradoxes of Deployment

1. ***Self-Reliance and Self-Sufficiency***

   India, since its independence, has pursued a policy of self-reliance. This has prompted the governments to build dams and set up heavy industries as well as consumer goods industries. Self-reliance is the ability to develop infrastructure. This has not been, however, accompanied by an ability to be self-sufficient in terms of technologies, equipment, finances, or manufacturing capacities. Self-reliance without self-sufficiency is of little use as it would still leave vast sections of population unattended in terms of its needs. There can be no greater formula for economic growth and social equity than achieving self-sufficiency with self-reliance.

2. ***Self-Image and Self-Worth***

   All successful persons have an image of themselves. Their self-image prompts them to face the world and lead their teams with confidence. In a sense, self-image is a success enabler (as long as it does not lead to narcissism!). Yet, such self-image tends to be the preserve of only the exclusive few. On the other hand, every person can, and must, have self-worth. Whatever be the avocation one is in, or the activity one chooses to do, one must take pride in executing it to the fullest capability. This leads one to a strong sense of self-worth. Self-image that is backed by self-worth is a sustainable alchemy, not only for the individual but also for the broader organization.

3. ***Managing and Leading***

   Managing is the process of running a business. Leading is the process of taking a business to a new horizon. From a time not so long ago when management was considered all-encompassing, we are now in a stage when managing is considered separate from (and unfortunately, somewhat inferior to) leading. Also, it is considered that management is a task of a lower hierarchy and leadership is one of a higher hierarchy. This not-so-discerning differentiation is misconceived. Leading is the sole purpose of management. A manager who cannot be a leader cannot be a true manager. A leader who cannot manage cannot be a good leader. The process of running a business perforce must also lead the business to consistently better results.

4. ***Empowering and Enabling***

   Leadership (and management) is no longer about just controlling and coordinating. It is more about inspiring and influencing. Frequently used in that context is "empowerment" as a concept. It is felt that leaders and managers should empower their team members to be able to accomplish the goals on their own. Empowerment is provision of more authority on one's life and conduct. More than this oft-used cliché, the real requirement for leaders and managers is to enable their team members to set and accomplish their own goals. "Enabling" is making it possible for someone to achieve something by creating certain necessary conditions; this must include, among others, empowerment too. Enabling clearly is a more appropriate concept than just empowerment.

5. ***Title and Stature***

   A key feature of social evolution, over centuries, has been the emergence of titles. Titles signify the ranks in a profession or in a society. Titles have such compelling attraction that everyone seeks them. Titles tend to be for a few. In comparison, stature is the importance and respect that a person has because of his or her ability and achievement. While titles can be had only by a few (and ironically, bestowed at times independent of stature), stature can be gained by all independent of their hierarchy through sheer dint of achievements and accomplishments. Virtuous individuals and organizations aspire to acquire stature rather than seek ranks.

When "Second" is "First"

Many times, in the pursuit of visible results or even in the conduct of activities, the central purpose becomes lost in visibility. The preoccupation with the results and activities makes one equate the very act or the result (like teaching or qualification) to be the same as the purpose (like learning or education), respectively. This makes achievements rather mechanical, suboptimizing capabilities and creativity. The organizational designs, including structures and processes, as well as individual and social systems (including values and ethics) must focus on the underlying core purpose. Playing a sport or participating in a competition is more important than winning the game or scoring in the competition. Similarly, putting in the best effort without aspiring for a result is philosophically more appropriate. The spirit is considered more relevant than success, and the effort more relevant than result. That said, if in the ten aspects of life that have been discussed above, the primary driver of progress is recognized and followed, spirit will soar high as much as success will sustain for sure.

Chapter 20

Time as a Resource

In human life, time is the most universal but also the most limited resource, making time unique and precious. From the time one is born to the time one breathes one's last, time is the constant companion of one's life. One ought to be conscious of this once the cognitive abilities start developing but unfortunately few accord the importance to time as one must. The importance of time in acquiring education, gaining experience, developing relationships, promoting careers, preserving health, and delaying aging is well known. Yet, how to deploy and utilize "unit time" as a resource for maximal efficiency and effectiveness is a highly personal matter, varying from individual to individual and family to family.

Approach to time is a core value that one imbibes based on one's family, educational, and experiential backgrounds. It is not unusual for kids to watch their parents, siblings, and relatives at work and in personal life, and imbibe certain values about the use of time. Likewise, the educational systems of the institution a person joins and the approaches of friends in the educational and social circles further supplement the approaches to time. Over time, a person develops an approach towards life that could be structured and systematic, flexible and tactical, or fatalistic and philosophical. Depending on which of the three approaches govern a person's view of life, his or her attitude towards time also would vary. These approaches to life are not usually static and could vary with phases in life. Accordingly, one's approaches to utilization of time would also vary. Though this chapter is not about approaches to life, some discussion on the topic would be in order.

Approaches to Life and Time

A structured and systematic approach to life is the ultimate remit of a planner or a productivity expert. This person is an industrial engineering expert of sorts, knowing exactly what should be done when, how, and why. Obviously, a structured and systematic person knows the value of time the best. He or she considers life as a duty to be fulfilled diligently and efficiently. A flexible and tactical approach to life involves sizing up each activity as it emerges and responding to it, based on perceptions of risk and reward for each activity and the modality/time for fulfilling it. The flexible and tactical person seeks to manage life for happiness than be managed by it as a duty. A fatalistic and philosophical approach to life follows a minimalist and mindful approach to life without exerting effort to seek more than what follows from circumstances. The fatalistic and philosophical person seeks nothing other than emotional fulfilment from life. Figure 20.1 presents the three approaches to life and time.

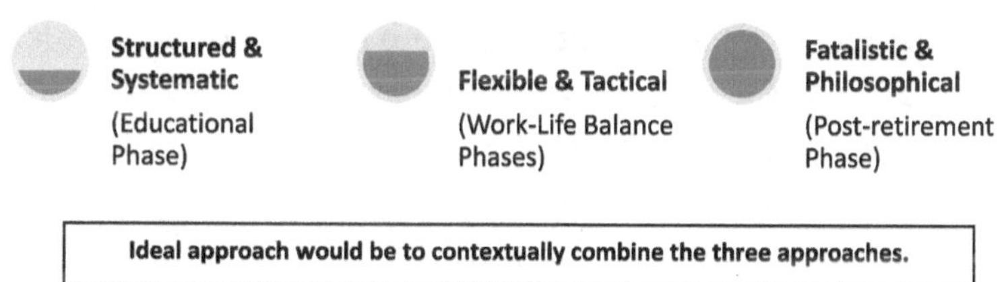

Figure 20.1: Three Approaches to Life & Time

Typically, during the educational phase of life, a person is likely to be and expected to be structured and systematic. As one takes up a career, he starts appreciating the utility of a structured and systematic approach to life but also starts understanding the opportunistic benefits of being tactical and flexible. Somewhere during the journey, and certainly after retirement from active service, he starts giving up being in the race of life and begins to appreciate the fulfilment of being fatalistic and philosophical in life. An ideal calibration could be to see a phase-in of the three approaches as being sequential. These approaches are not mutually exclusive. A fatalistic and philosophical person may still be quite ordered and disciplined as to how he conducts his daily chores. As one struggles in career despite being structured or tactical, one may begin appreciating the benefits of being philosophical. It is easy to appreciate that the approach to life influences one's approach to time.

Time Erodes

Time ticks away relentlessly and perpetually all through one's life but one can try to gain a little by trying to live longer, and by living healthier without wastage of time. That said, whenever it occurs to one's mind, time erosion as a concept would hit one like a sudden fall of a ton of bricks. People respond to this realization with a variety of emotions: from frustration and desperation on one hand to recovery and urgency on the other. The former is counterproductive, whereas the latter could produce certain results. Both the types of responses lead to needless stress, and if encountered continuously accelerate the aging of individuals. That time dissolves relentlessly on its own is a truism. However, if we fail to make good use of time and create value in the process, negative emotions and stress are not the solutions; improved learning and enhanced productivity would be the right solutions.

Learning requires additional time even as the pressure of lost time mounts. That is where time management as a concept comes up. By decluttering activities, listing the uncluttered ones, prioritizing them, and even delisting the low-priority, non-value-adding ones, one would be able to have at one's disposal more time in a day than lost. Time thus released can be utilized to learn and carry out things more productively. Structured and systematic people, even when disrupted by unanticipated pressures and tempted by opportunistic incentives, can overcome erosion of time with the above approach. There is, however, a more meaningful approach to understand the true value of time, as an eternal clock. Life may freeze but time shall never freeze. Therein lies the great awakening.

Time as Continuous Refill

We know the sand-filled hourglass as the classic depiction, and as a well-engineered a classic measurement, of time. While time for an individual may be limited, time as an absolute resource is indeed timeless. The way to look at time is not to be agitated that time is getting lost continuously but also to be excited that time is getting continuously refilled. In fact, compared to any other resource, time is the only resource that gets continuously refilled. For example, when we expend money, it will not be automatically recouped unless specifically earned. On the other hand, even if we expend time, we can be sure that the next unit of time will be available to be utilized. Time is, therefore, a continuous refill to be positive and optimistic about. If we are unable to perform certain activity in each period of time, it can be performed soon after.

The concept of time as continuous refill is not meant to cause complacency. In fact, it is worthwhile for all of us to keep time logs to keep an account of time we spend on different activities such as priority activities or vital–essential–desirable activities, and to validate if the time has been spent productively or wastefully. By linking the time log to results in terms of fulfilment, happiness, and satisfaction, we could become even better on linking time to our emotional wellbeing. This exercise is an individual choice as each one's goals, schedules, and approaches vary. Many people in working life believe that "busyness" makes good business. Research has established that doing nothing and concentrating mind on serene matters helps improve productivity. The greatest support for this approach comes from the fact that the moment a rejuvenated person is ready to take on work again, time will be at hand. Figure 20.2 proposes an approach to cope with loss of time.

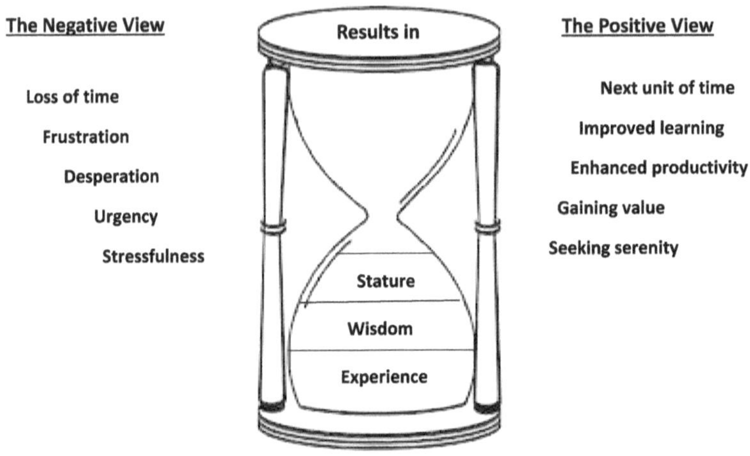

Figure 20.2: Coping with Loss of Time

Invisible Accumulation

Whether one is productively work-focused or meditatively leisure-focused, even as time ticks by something of value invisibly accumulates. That accumulation takes place in three categories: experience, wisdom, and stature. Experience helps one manage time effectively along with other resources. Experience helps one to come up with the right recipe for mixing resources in a time-effective manner for achieving desired results. Wisdom helps one identify whether certain endeavours are worth the while at all or those facing neglect are the ones that need to be picked up right away. Experience and wisdom together help a person in accomplishing results in a more effective manner than others could. Several such accomplishments based on experience and wisdom lead to stature. Stature again is not something that can be metricized; it is also an invisible accumulation that can be only felt by others.

Accumulation of experience, wisdom, and stature ideally must remain a silent phenomenon. It is a completely personal achievement that is related to one's approaches to life and time as discussed so far. Any public display by an individual on what he or she perceives as his or her wisdom and stature would only erode those invisible assets. There is reference in Hindu mythology to mystic powers that are developed based on continuous prayers and penances that must be utilized, if at all, for good causes in a discrete manner. Utilization on inappropriate matters and boastful references to such powers are said to lead to dramatic dilution of such powers. Invisibly accumulated experience, wisdom, and stature are akin to this. Interestingly, those who are experienced, wise, and statured realize the importance of time, and its judicious use in vesting them with such invisible accumulation.

Kala Chakra

As understood so far, a typical accomplished person who is blessed to reaching his or her full wisdom and stature in his or her sixties, is also ordained to lose the faculties progressively as he or she physically and intellectually declines with age. If one were to see this evolution as wisdom and stature traveling with time, the apogee is reached after six or more decades but thereafter when it gets down, the final perigee varies with the individual, given (a) the low and uncertain longevity, and (b) the differences in longevity. However, with the increased longevity of humans, the journey from apogee to low point can no longer be taken as an inconsequential, immaterial, and natural decline. On the other hand, with increasing longevity, there is an increasing need to preserve, if not enhance, the invisible accumulation.

As humanity moves forward on better physical health (with more advanced healthcare and nutrition), the need for better emotional health becomes self-evident. The approaches to life and time discussed in this chapter—namely, structured and systematic, flexible and tactical, fatalistic and philosophical—continue to be relevant over a much longer time horizon, even beyond the sixties. The need to think of time more as a refilling resource than as an eroding resource is more important than ever in the current context of information explosion through the Internet and social media. Once the perspectives outlined in this chapter are absorbed, the need to nurture the silent accumulation of experience, wisdom, and stature becomes self-evident. The wheel of time that starts from the first breath will keep spinning till the last breath of a human. It is entirely up to everyone to govern the speed to apogee and thereafter!

Chapter 21

Friends in Need

Organizations are groups of employees. Given the shared goals and objectives, one may hypothesize that friendly employees could provide the power of synergy to the organization. As the dictionary defines, friends are those who are not connected by family relationships but who have mutual attachment and affection for each other. Every individual as he or she grows in life relies on friends and friendship to seek support, guidance, and fulfilment beyond the family. Close friendship has a sublime and overarching impact on one's life, with friends being relied upon for thoughts, actions, and guidance that even the family members or professional colleagues cannot offer. Friendship that starts from childhood tends to be a lifelong friendship. It is, however, possible that friendship between adults based on mutual respect, affection, and caring could also emerge as a lifetime development.

A true friend understands and fulfils the needs of the other, without the other ever having to express. True friendship never seeks reciprocity; it is also not an accounting transaction of 'give and take,' on any dimension. Need fulfilment is the key to one's equanimity with life. Upbringing, education, and experience teach one to seek needs, fulfil the needs, and moderate them. The unpredictability and harshness of life, however, makes individuals dependent on their friends for need fulfilment. This could be as commonplace as material support, as appropriate as intellectual support, and as sublime as emotional support. The unbelievable growth of social networking points to the omniscience of friendship as a fundamental trigger of life. Not all human needs can be easily and effectively fulfilled, however. Many times, they require extraordinary understanding, patience, persistence, and courage. Need fulfilment by a true friend is, therefore, a selfless act that seeks no name or fame, and would even accept suffering and sacrifice. No wonder then that the adage says that a friend in need is a friend indeed.

Maslow's Need Hierarchy (or Pyramid)

If need fulfilment is the foundation of friendship, one may analyse the framework of human needs to examine the nexus between need fulfilment and friendship development. Amongst all the theories of needs, Abraham Maslow's theory ranks high. In 1943, Abraham Maslow's article "A Theory of Human Motivation" that appeared in Psychological Review proposed five basic sets of human needs, which were further expanded upon in his book "Toward a Psychology of Being." Abraham Maslow attempted to formulate a needs-based framework of human motivation based upon his clinical experiences with humans. He did not base his theory on prior psychology theories of his day from leaders in the field of psychology such as Freud and Skinner that were largely theoretical or based upon animal behaviour. Very quickly, Maslow's need hierarchy became a major foundation of organizational motivation theories.

Maslow proposed the need hierarchy as comprising physiological, safety, social, esteem, and self-actualization needs. This hierarchy is a pyramid of needs, with many physiological needs serving as the base of the pyramid, and the self-actualization needs serving as the apex. Safety, social, and esteem needs form the mid-tier needs. The basis of Maslow's theory of motivation is that human beings are motivated by unsatisfied needs, and that certain lower-order needs must be satisfied before higher-order needs can be addressed. According to the teachings of Abraham Maslow, the general needs (physiological, safety, love, and esteem) must be fulfilled before a person is able to act unselfishly. He believed that once a lower level of need is fulfilled, the human being seeks a higher level of need, and the lower level of need no longer motivates him or her.

Friendship Through Inverted Need Pyramid

True friendship follows an inverted pyramid, wherein it provides self-actualization ahead of any other deficit need of a person. A true friend helps the other realize his or her true intrinsic potential. A true friend of a person understands the capabilities of the person to soar higher but that need support. The true friend provides the needed encouragement and intellectual support to help his friend realize the full potential of the capabilities. In the good old days of school and college education, it was not unusual for the more endowed to help the less brilliant classmate bridge the knowledge gaps. True friends also complement, synergizing each other's strengths and helping each other overcome the respective weaknesses.

Self-actualization, in an ecosystem of friendship, has been the foundation of many entrepreneurial journeys. While the friendship foundations of global corporations such as Microsoft, Sony, Apple, and Google are well known, there are examples in India too. In the South Indian movie industry, ace producer Nagi Reddy and creative writer Chakrapani were two friends who founded and nurtured the vast Vijaya production house through an amazing bond of friendship and complementarity. The friendship foundations of Infosys are also well known. Figure 21.1 presents the inverted hierarchy of friendship needs, taking the example of a typical start-up.

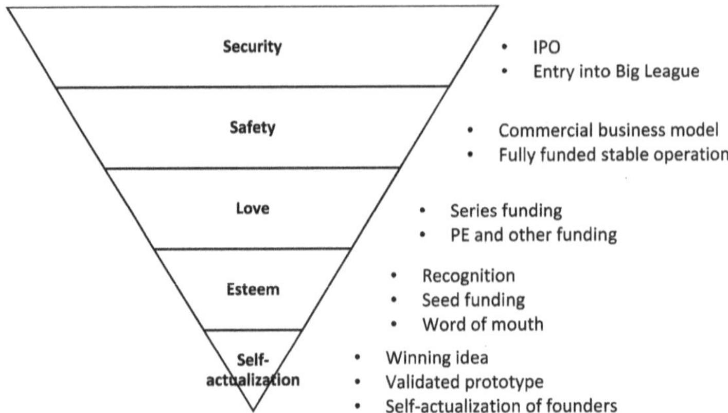

Figure 21.1: The Inverted Hierarchy of Friendship Needs: A Start-up Example

True friendship seeks no esteem. There is perhaps no better description of esteem-free friendship than the friendship of Lord Krishna and the poor, humble Kuchela in the Hindu mythology. A true friend never looks at his or her friends through a lens of esteem. Nor does he ever forget his humble origins or the friends of humble origins. In true friendship, material issues do not colour or influence the approach towards each other. True friendship, as known in earlier generations, was never viral; nor was it in the mode of mass socialization. The infectious friendship fever of today's social network sites is an instantaneous steroid but lacks the lasting emotional connect of yesteryears' true and close friendship. Yet, there exist positive episodes of instant social connectivity over Facebook, and Twitter, which have saved lives and promoted noble causes.

Personal knowledge of each other is not a sine qua non to help in friendly causes in these contemporary times. That true friendship provides safety and security goes without saying. The assurance that friends provide often encourages talented and indigent people find their mark. The role of true friendship in looking after the needy in terms of their physiological needs is also remarkable. Sharing of what one has with the other provides pure joy to both the giver and receiver. Many movie moguls and business magnates passionately recall how the shelter and food provided by others provided sustenance and optimism to stay on in the pursuit of seemingly difficult goals. The ability to give a break to a friend in life is a vital characteristic of friendship. Instances abound of right introductions helping capable people achieve exceptional, yet highly deserved, transformations in life. Figure 21.2 presents the model of overlapping friendship circles.

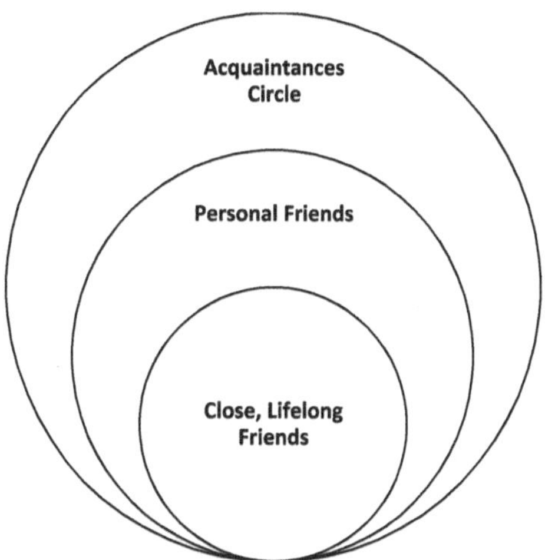

Figure 21.2: A Model of Overlapping Friendship Circles

Friendship Circles

Typically, friendship is a canvas of expanding and intersecting or overlapping circles as shown. One typically has, in the outermost circle, all the acquaintances. People in that outermost circle feel obliged, rather than intrinsically motivated, to keep track of each other's progress periodically. Many a time, they are connected through social networking sites, and the real emotions and the true vibes are never likely to be known. This may be called the acquaintance circle. The next inner circle is the circle of friends who have personally experienced the attributes of each other and had been part of life's journeys in schools, colleges, and professions. Typically, this circle is nurtured by a feeling of happiness with each other's progress, and conversely unhappiness with any setbacks. This is the most visible form of friendship circle. The smallest or innermost circle, however, represents the core of close, lifelong, and lifetime friends. Friends in this circle literally think and live for each other, with perfect alignment in intentions, thoughts, expressions, and actions.

One should be considered blessed if one has at least one friend in the innermost lifetime friendship circle. Ideally, the three circles should be overlapping. This leads to an orderly development of friendship structures. Intuitively, introverts would have minimalist circles and extroverts expansive circles. However, an introvert could draw many extroverts into his fold, and vice versa. Also, friendship is a matter of the heart and the mind, and sacrifice in friendship is additionally a matter of the gut. The human heart, mind, and gut are capable of multiple emotions and intentions; hence, it is possible for friends, as they grow up in life, to be in any of the three circles. As one matures, however, life teaches that true friendship cannot be built on one dimension, and requires alignment on several human attributes, including values. The soft and sensitive attributes of pious, caring, compassionate, affectionate, and positive living mark the ultimate definition of the innermost lifetime friendship circle. It is an existence of sublime purity to discover the blissful joy of a blessed life.

Chapter 22

Connected Contentment

Organizations are set up to deliver through employees. The classical theory of organizational delivery hinges around employee motivation. Organizations deliver in an optimal manner when people in the organizations are motivated to perform. Motivation occurs when people feel fulfilled. Fulfilment occurs at two levels: first, when people feel that their achievements meet or exceed their aspirations, and second, when their achievements are recognized and rewarded. Recognitions and rewards occur, from an organizational perspective, at two levels: first when the aspirations of the people are aligned to organizational goals, and second when organizational goals are met through individual and team achievements. All the above are hypotheses and perceptions, and not commonplace organizational realities.

There is a more fundamental paradigm of organizational delivery that focuses on natural ways of human contentment and connectivity. What we have in organization–people interactions are a complex maze of perceptions and realities. The mismatch of perceptions and realities and of facts and imagery leads to turbulence in organizations marked by demotivated employees, failing performance, missed goals, and relative dissatisfaction of both people and organizations. This negative circle is detrimental to the productivity and delivery of organizations. The root causes are complex and often invisible and cannot be managed by planned interventions such as performance management or people development. This chapter proposes that there is a more fundamental foundation than motivation that all organizations must aspire for to achieve the best levels of productivity and delivery in a natural manner.

Contented and Connected

Organizations are the platforms for collaboration amongst their people constituencies. Without genuine and effective collaboration, organizations cannot deliver to their full potential; they may not even survive the competition. Collaboration in an organization requires that its people are contended and connected. This paradigm of collaborative connectivity is contrasted by what is normally found in practice in organizations that are filled by individualized approaches; this may be called competitive individuality. The former paradigm of collaborative connectivity is based on the positive principles of human psychology as well as oriental spirituality that reflect two essential characteristics: first, one must be at peace with oneself as well as the environment, and the second, one must stay connected with one's inner self and the outer world through introspection.

The latter paradigm of motivated individuality is based on the principles of modern management and western social thought that reflect two essential characteristics: first, one can and must go beyond the natural comfort zone to deliver and earn rewards, and the second, people must fundamentally be organized through formal structures and systems of the rational mind. It is easy to see the difference between the two paradigms. The first is self-administered, whereas the second is externally imposed, from an individual's perspective. The second paradigm draws its sustenance from various motivational theories, starting from the Hawthorne studies, and needs constant external attention for sustainability. In fact, the second paradigm is not even truly sustainable as it collapses without external props. The first paradigm, on the other hand, draws inspiration from within, and therefore is truly sustainable. There are fundamental differences between the paradigms, however. The first paradigm requires a relatively well-rounded personality brought up with less of materialism and more of spiritualism. Obviously, in today's world, this has been taken up as a motto only by a few enlightened institutions. The second paradigm works with any personality that is prompted by materialism and relativism. Obviously again, most institutions find it expedient to shape personalities on material and competitive quests.

Contentment Versus Motivation

Being contented is the state of being happy with what one has and what one achieves. It may seem to be a retro theme to suggest that people in the organization should be contended rather than motivated. Being motivated means being driven by a factor or a combination of factors beyond the natural behaviour to perform and seek rewards. In a classic sense, motivation suggests a factored drive-in of performance, whereas contentment suggests a status quo with what one has. The difference between the two concepts is, however, more than semantic. Motivation as a driver is intrinsically materialistic and artificial and is also stress-producing. Motivation is an affected behaviour of people seeking constant fulfilment beyond what a human being needs. Contentment, on the other hand, is intrinsically spiritual and natural, and is stress relieving. Contentment is an intrinsic behaviour of people that is both psychological and biological. For example, when one becomes hungry, one tends to become contented once the hunger is satiated. On the other hand, a motivated individual driven only by rewards cannot stop seeking materialistic fulfilment even if it is far beyond what his or her life needs.

Contentment, as an oriental principle of life, teaches people to find happiness in what one can find in life. It dissuades people from seeking a utopian world. Given the imperfections that could occur in man-made organizations, contentment helps one to attain equanimity in the face of several stress-producing challenges. Motivation, as a Western principle of management, exhorts people to look beyond the base without exploring how the base itself can be intrinsically reinforced. Motivation in some ways is like a superstructure built on weak foundations. In matters of human physical health, immunity and prophylactic approaches to wellness are far more effective and enduring as well as less costly than pharmaceutical therapeutic approaches to treating illness. In matters of organizational behavioural health too, for bettering performance, resilience and perseverance approaches to high performance are far more effective, enduring, and effortless than motivation-based rewards. Figure 22.1 presents a model of the virtuous organizational behaviour based on contented connectivity and motivated individuality.

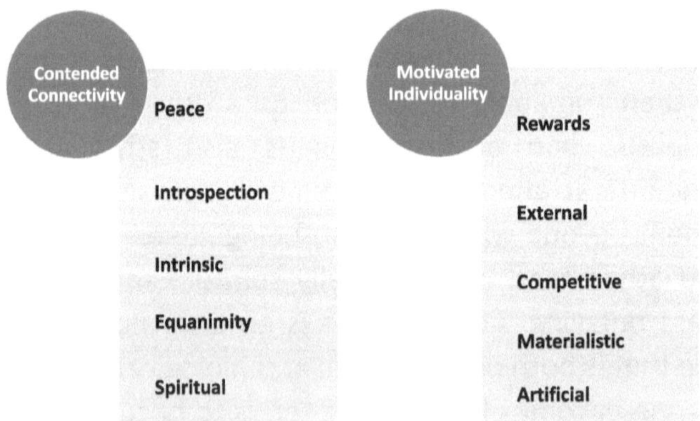

Figure 22.1: The Virtuous Organizational Behaviour

Connected, despite Specialized

The modern organization owes its structures and processes to the concept of specialization. Specialization has been the foundation of the evolution of civilization whether it was functionally established (for example, musician, teacher), socially established (for example, royalty, military), or religiously indoctrinated (for example, the Hindu Temple and Mutt systems or the Christian Church and Vatican systems). Specialization helped in deepening of knowledge and excelling of practice in the domains, but it also led to the formation of barriers between the various specializations. This has led to functional, social, and religious stresses resulting in volatility in the development of humanity. It is not surprising that organizations had to be formed based on specializations, but it is certainly concerning that specialization has led to silo formation in organizations. As a result, much like in the case of motivation, organizations resort to various internal and external forums to connect silos. Just as an unenlightened individual believes that he or she is distinct and differentiated in the universe, an individual who is dogmatic in specialization fails to see himself or herself as a part of the organization.

A connected organizational ethos helps functions deliver organizational goals effectively. As illustrated in Figure 22.2, the foundations of organizational connectivity occur at two levels, one individual and the other functional. The connected individual believes that he or she exists in communion with his or her inner self and in connectivity with every other individual. He or she recognizes that both in gross and subtle manners, his or her existence impacts and is impacted by the presence and absence of other organizational members. The connectivity of functions is also viewed and shaped by individuals from their individual lenses. An unconnected individual is blinded to the relevance and importance of the other functions, and to that extent, fails to grow beyond his or basic core function. In the organizational setting as in the social milieu, there is no alternative to staying connected while being specialized. The relative success of residential schools and campuses is due to the connectivity such residential life enforces on the residents. The success of the mammoth public sector units such as steel plants in the post-independence India has been largely due to the residential townships and the related connectivity that helped improve individual and functional connectivity.

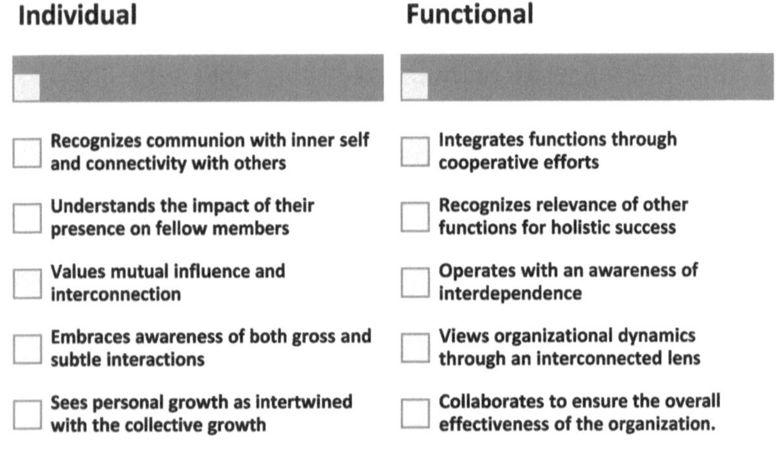

Figure 22.2: The Foundations of Organizational Connectivity

Contended Connectivity, the Natural Way

An organization with contended and connected people would ipso facto be a stress-free and happy organization. But would it be an efficient and effective organization without the commonly used motivational and specialization tools? The answer lies in preparing the individuals to understand themselves in a holistic fashion from their childhood through the schools and colleges. While it should be the responsibility of homes and families to teach children good values in the socio-religious context, it must be the responsibility of schools and colleges to teach how an individual can reach contentment and connection by discovering one's complete self. From overcoming physical and mental limitations to reaching the full potential of one's body and brain cells, collaborative actualization should be a part of the curriculums both at school and college levels. An intrinsic personal awareness and execution process based on self-discovery, duly aided by such teachings, brings in contentment without any artificial props of motivation. And a person who is in equanimity with himself or herself stays connected internally and externally.

Organizations can reinforce the contented connectivity paradigm by ensuring equality and equity in organizations. By being an equal opportunity employer and by being equitable in talent management, organizations can avoid the factors that induce stresses and strains in organizations. Lack of equity is a fundamental destabilizing factor that is sought to be countered by various motivational programs; this is much akin to symptomatic therapeutic programs that seek to treat illness. Leaders in organization, who experience and demonstrate ego states, whether by personality type or contextual state, are often impediments to the virtuous processes of contended connectivity. Development of executives, managers, and leaders from the grassroots level on the paradigm of contented connectivity is an essential need for organizational excellence. Recruitment of well-rounded mature individuals and enabling them to discover their full potential and fulfil them all through the careers is a sustainable strategy to efficiency and effectiveness in organizations. Contentment and connectivity of people would make organizations communities of happiness as much as epitomes of delivery.

Chapter 23

Balance in Life

Fun at work is a contemporary motto in today's organizations. These are especially marked by happiness, bordering on liberation. Birthday celebrations take the cake, literally and figuratively. Modern-day team members like to chill out, notwithstanding the stresses and strains as well as trials and tribulations they may have experienced thus far in their lives. The celebrations do provide momentary relief to people before they return to a life of dreary routine or exciting challenge. Amidst the fun and frolic, one must realize that everyone has grown one year older, and hopefully thus everyone has also grown one year wiser. Quite apart from what the anniversaries signify as a reminder of graceful aging, there is a need to evolve a model of life in terms of time and talent. An earlier chapter discussed a novel view of time as a refillable resource, even though each second lost is a second lost forever.

The refillable proposition is a motivational theorem for people not to brood over time that is lost and instead focus on what lies ahead. That said, it is an inexorable fact of life that time is a factor of perpetual loss. Human beings have limited life spans that are influenced by genetics and lifestyles. Corporations, on the other hand, can have an indefinite life, threatened only by reckless mismanagement, discontinuities in environment, and exacerbation of competition. Time is, therefore, a finite commodity both for people and corporations that keeps ticking remorselessly. As time flies by, it also fortunately bestows a few gains on the individuals and corporations essentially as the former are genetically wired to learn and the latter are humanly designed to learn. The balance of life is thus one of balance of perpetual loss of time and perpetual gain of time. This chapter discusses some underlying concepts and provides a potentially relevant construct that could help individuals, entities, and societies.

Perpetual Loss of Time

Managing time is a subject of many prescriptions. From handbooks to productivity courses, there exist multiple tips and methodologies to optimize the use of time. Time management, however, needs a holistic paradigm that has for the individual as well as the organization clear life philosophies, strategic plans, work plans, and execution agenda. Day-to-day time management stems from the clarity one has on the above paradigm. Following through, the key to following any tip, methodology, or paradigm must be an awareness of the inexorable and unstoppable way time ticks away. This recognition must be accompanied by a mature response that balances available time on a host of daily activities classified as essential (for example, quality sleep, preparation, and exercise), value adding (for example, learning and working), desirable (for example, socialization), and individual (for example, personal hobbies). In contrast, being paranoid and miserly about time and adopting crash methodologies of conservation of time or frenetic pace of professional and personal life would be counterproductive.

Any sense of loss with respect to time needs to be related to a perspective of one's goals in life. There are actors and musicians who simultaneously accept many movies, sports persons who sign on multiple tournaments, and consultants who take on several assignments, all as if there would be no tomorrow. There are also actors, musicians, sports persons, and consultants who are very selective and sequential in what they accept. At one level such an approach reflects what each of them sees as each person's monetization goals in life. However, more fundamentally, such anxiety for monetization, or lack of it, reflects their perceptions on the value of time. It is not for nothing that the adage of "time is money" has come about. Loss of time makes no distinction between individuals and is completely out of one's control except to the extent of individual differences in utilization. That said, individuals and corporations have considerable leeway in ensuring that they offset the perpetual loss of time in an equally perpetual gainful manner. Figure 23.1 summarizes the understanding of loss and gain of time as a theme.

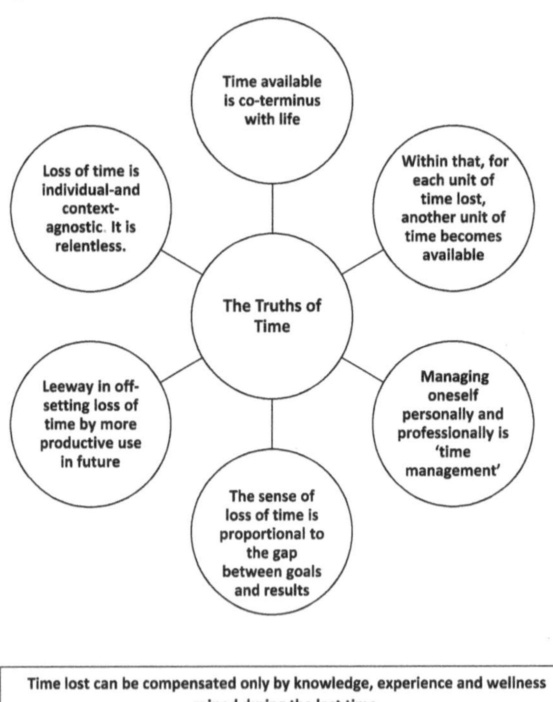

Figure 23.1: An Understanding of Loss and Gain of time

Perpetual Gain of Knowledge

Over time, with clearly set objectives, individuals and corporations can gain on knowledge. Wise people do not, therefore, rue over the unrelenting loss of time. Instead, they see time as an investment that helps achieve gains in knowledge. However, there is an inadequate appreciation of what knowledge means and how knowledge can be continuously acquired. Many people hold that knowledge can be substituted or supplanted by experience, intuition, and instinct. Such hypotheses are erroneous and are based on infirm foundations. Knowledge, holistically, is the understanding, information, skills, and capabilities one gains through education or experience. Knowledge is continuously absorbed and stored in the brain and processed and expressed through the mind. Intuition, and to a large extent instinct too, is the inner knowledge that is bestowed on a person through a sharp definition of his or her sensory faculties and a differentiated ability to synthesize perceptions and knowledge.

Clearly, knowledge is the foundation of any gainful achievement in life. Even those who understand this hypothesis often have misconceptions as to how knowledge is acquired. The most common fallacy is that the acquisition of knowledge plateaus after the collegiate education and the early years of experience. This is based on an erroneous institutional philosophy of learning that does not leverage how human beings are (or can be) inherently and perpetually wired to acquire knowledge. To be able to understand this, the five ways of acquiring knowledge need to be understood. These are: seeking–responding, awareness–understanding, learning–absorbing, experiencing–integrating, and observing–reinforcing. These five steps, unfortunately, are seen to be sequential or at best sporadically combined. This inadequate manner of acquiring knowledge limits the knowledge an individual can acquire relative to potential.

The Knowledge Loop

The primal way of generating and spreading knowledge is through seeking and responding. It is commonly assumed that this phase is best seen to be limited to the first baby months of a person. It is not so in reality. Even as one grows older, knowledge is developed through the "seek–receive" mechanism. A more evolved level of knowledge development is through the "awareness–understanding" bridge. This is, again, akin to toddlers and children becoming aware of several matters of life and understanding them through positive and negative outcomes. This, by no means, is only a child's way of knowledge gaining. Even mature persons need to gain awareness and understanding of new situations as they develop. Becoming aware of the new circumstances and developing an understanding helps build foundations of new knowledge even for knowledgeable persons.

Learning–absorbing is the more commonly appreciated method of knowledge acquisition, leading to formal degrees and certifications. Enormous emphasis is placed on this phase of knowledge acquisition as the degrees make a difference to the career entry. Society and organizations provide the ecosystems for people to experience and integrate. The same educational course taught in two countries would, even in these days of globalization, would be interpreted, absorbed, and acted upon in two different ways in the two nations. More specifically, in an organizational context, knowledge acquired through learning is upgraded, adapted, or honed through experience. And each organization can develop a unique competence in this regard. Each of the above four steps of knowledge acquisition involve external inputs. The fifth step of knowledge acquisition, "observing–reinforcing," is perhaps the only step of knowledge acquisition that is wholly individual-driven. This requires a person to be keenly observant and have the willingness to draw appropriate lessons from observations. Figure 23.2 presents the knowledge loop.

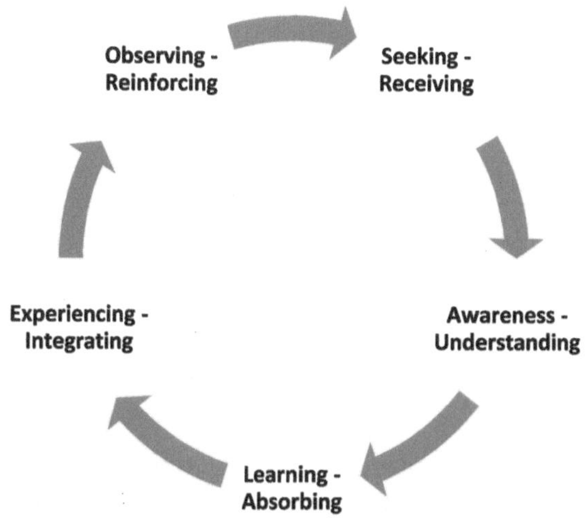

Figure 23.2: The Knowledge Loop

Knowledge – Every Moment, Every Way

Faced with the perpetual loss of time, competent individuals must strive to enhance knowledge every moment and in every way. The five-step knowledge loop discussed above provides a seamless methodology of continuous knowledge development, applicable for individuals as well as entities. The primal way of seeking–receiving becomes relevant whenever an individual faces an uncertain ecosystem. Rather than be overawed, the individual must seek attention and demand response. The natural way of awareness–understanding requires a calm and analytical state of mind that absorbs verbal and nonverbal cues and understands the supporting notions. The formal manner of learning–absorbing is often seen as an activity for a formal degree. True knowledge acquisition occurs when the knowledge seeker and knowledge giver focus on "know-why" behind each nugget of knowledge. This approach prepares one to apply or customize the acquired knowledge to multiple industry situations.

Experiencing–integrating is another aspect of continuous formal learning. While all societies and entities provide scope for experiential learning, certain organizations and societies provide their members immersive experiences that stick to their minds with deep insights. Organizations that have formal systems of mentoring in organizations (for example, Japanese companies), and societies that are blessed with model disseminators of knowledge (for example, active and positive media) provide beneficial knowledge arising out of day-to-day developments. Ultimately, it is for individuals and corporations to recognize the importance of observation and reinforcement. The observant individual reinforces knowledge from every activity he or she observes—whether the activity is performed by a superior, peer, or subordinate, whether the activity pertains to his or her domain or someone else's, or if the activity is a corporate business activity or civil society activity. As an old saying goes, nothing is trivial in terms of the knowledge such seeming triviality can impart.

Knowledge Corporations, Societies

Observant corporations, in a similar manner, do not stay still in knowledge; they endeavour to be knowledge corporations. They seek attention and receive knowledge. They provide opportunities for individuals to reflect and develop an understanding of people and processes. They emphasize the induction of personnel with excellent knowledge credentials and nurture a pioneering atmosphere of learning in an organization. They institutionalize a culture of generating knowledge through every activity of an organization. Most importantly, they sustain the spirit of inquisitiveness and curiosity in individuals. As an extension of such a knowledge-driven mindset, corporations themselves continuously seek attention and responses in the wake of uncertainty, enhance awareness and understanding of emerging environments, learn to develop new products and processes, integrate experiences for greater knowledge, and observe other corporations to reinforce their own competitive positions.

Knowledge societies have existed from times immemorial. The tides of history have swept away some knowledge societies, battered some, reconstructed some, and created some others. All through the torments of history, it is amazing how knowledge survived and grew overall. Societies that have been both diligent and fortunate to preserve and develop knowledge have prospered or are on their way to prosperity. India needs to consider how the nation can recapture its ancient glory of being a knowledge society; a society that gave the world's richest religion multiple scriptures and epics that set forth principles of living relevant even today, a society that computed, without the aid of any computing devices, all the planetary movements that are accurate to the second even compared to the current days of atomic clock, a society that gave natural healing through Ayurveda and Yoga that stay relevant in the face of strides in synthetic medicine, and a society that built cradles of knowledge such as Nalanda and Nagarjuna Sagar centuries ago. As India reinvents itself towards economic supremacy, it is not a race against time, but it is the pace of ageless knowledge creation that would determine India's success.

Chapter 24

Towards Destressing

Stress has emerged as an important characteristic of contemporary living. Many medical experts consider that stress, with its collateral outcomes, has been a major contributor for metabolic disorders and psychosomatic diseases. However, some experts also believe that a certain level of stress is required for an individual to perform at his or her full potential. Whatever be the validity of either of the concepts (on an individualized rather than a genericized format), it would certainly be better if one's full potential is achieved without stressing oneself. To appreciate this, one needs to delve into the real meaning of stress. Stress is pressure or worry on a person caused by problems and difficulties in life.

Stressed individuals suffer by themselves, fighting unseen (and unnecessary) battles with invisible (and unreal) enemies. Sadly, and inevitably, they also cause suffering by causing stress in, and to, their families and teams. There is a debate whether such perceptions of stress are real or self-inflicted. CNN carried a valuable analysis of stress as a new universal phenomenon and approaches to cope with it. (http://www.cnn.com/2014/11/19/health/stress-free-acceptance). It considers stress as an internal factor that can be moderated by the individual rather than blamed on circumstances imposed on the individual externally. A central theme of the article is that pleasure or pain, joy or sorrow, and peace or stress are not found in external objects or beings but instead are found in the relationship one has with those things. The article also makes an important point. One's relationship with the world is entirely dependent on the nature of one's inner personality, which comprises the mind and the intellect. Figure 24.1 illustrates the characteristics of intellectual strength which are discussed below.

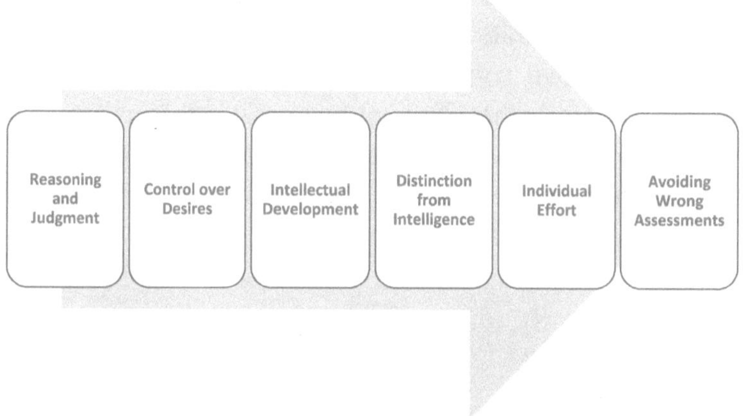

Figure 24.1: Characteristics of Intellectual Strength

According to the CNN article, the mind desires and feels while the intellect reasons, judges, and decides. Stress is generated when the intellect loses control over the mind's desires. The article hypothesizes that the fundamental requirement for a stress-free life is to develop a strong intellect and control desires. The article also emphasizes that intellectual strength is distinct and different from intelligence. Any amount of intelligence, which is knowledge acquired from external sources cannot, per se, develop one's intellect. Intellect can only be developed by individual effort through exercising one's faculty of questioning and reasoning. Wrong assessments of the external world are also proposed as an important cause of stress. I commend the cited CNN article, which reads and feels almost like the Hindu spiritual philosophy, as a must-read for its simplicity and relevance in understanding individual and organizational behaviour. That said, the capitalistic, competitive, and volatile nature of the contemporary world makes it necessary for individuals to have attributes that can help them avoid or manage their stress, should the above spiritual approach be not followed. This chapter proposes that individuals must try to develop five pairs of attributes that could help them avoid difficulties and worries in life. These attributes are: aspirational and adaptive, aware and academic, alert and attentive, communicative and corrective, and primal and philosophical. These cannot be useful individually or even as single pairs; they are effective only as a holistic combination of all the five pairs. Figure 24.2 presents the framework for stress-free living.

Figure 24.2: A Framework for Stress-free Living

Aspirational and Adaptive

Aspiration is at the root of human behaviour. Some individuals are bold or blasé enough to declare their aspirations, whereas some are reticent and circumspect to do so. Aspirational means wanting very much to achieve success in one's career or to improve the social status or standard of living. Stress gets generated as one works to achieve aspirations, more so against odds. When achievements trail aspirations, a debilitating circle of increasing stress comes into play. All aspirants tend to choose certain means to achieve their aspirations but somewhere along the route miss the wood for the trees. Take the case of students who aspire to join an elite educational institution, in India or abroad. They typically miss the point that acquiring academic excellence regardless of the institution is more important than wanting to join the elite institution or losing motivation when the admission is missed. Same is the case of professionals who seek to join top rung corporations; in the process, they miss their own ability to impact positively any institution they are eventually able to join with the right professional skills.

Aspiration must be accompanied by the adaptive attribute. Adaptive means being able to change when necessary to deal with different situations. Adaptive does not mean succumbing, however. Individuals as well as organizations frequently encounter situations quite different from those envisaged when they would tune in and scale up their aspirations. Being adaptive does not mean scaling down aspirations. The boom in shale gas does not mean that the CEO of a crude oil behemoth must give up on the established core. It, however, requires being adaptive to retool the strategy in favour of shale gas exploitation or invest in shale companies as a hedging strategy. Development of new cost-effective shale oil exploration technologies such as fracking may be relevant in either case. The ability to be aspirational and adaptive comes from an ability to be aware and academic.

Aware and Academic

Stress is generated when people get into situations without the requisite knowledge or capability to handle. Smokers who are unaware of the dangers of tobacco or people who are unaware of the deleterious effects of junk food are just examples of how individuals who rely on them for stress relief would eventually be stressed out because of the resultant ill health. Being aware means knowing and realizing something, for the good or for the bad. Awareness is the basic minimum attribute of an individual or an organization that saves a situation. Lack of basic awareness leads to considerable stress as one would get into situations, the gravity, or requirements of which one does not simply know. An individual, for example, needs to be, at the minimum, aware that handling chemicals could be dangerous. The awareness would lead to a reference to the knowledgeable experts who can advise on the dangerous chemical reactions and the ways to avoid or control them. Being aware is the first step to being adaptive. Adaptive behaviour, especially to changing environments, eliminates or reduces many causes of stress. Awareness needs access to expertise to be meaningful. Awareness will come to naught if it is accompanied by defiance. Awareness must be accompanied by openness.

Expertise comes from ceaseless academic quest. Being academic means reading, studying, experimenting, or conducting research to enhance knowledge. Plastic has been a wonder material that ushered in a revolution in the consumer goods and food processing industries, from the time of its launch. Yet, only subsequent academic studies, decades later, could bring out the harmful effects of certain types of plastics and the ingredients that are used in plastic manufacture (or which remain in the plastic products). Today, growing usage and indiscriminate discarding of plastics has become such a global concern of pollution that the World Environment Day in 2018 was dedicated to curbing the consumption of plastics. Whether it is the harmful effects of tobacco and alcohol or the beneficial effects of herbs and spices, all agrarian in origin, academic development continues to identify new problems, provide new solutions, or revalidate ancient knowledge. By being aware generically on a broad spectrum and being academic in the chosen profession through continuous learning, one would be in greater command of one's career and life. As the CNN article points out, however, knowledge and intelligence by themselves are of little use without application, which requires one to be alert and attentive.

Alert and Attentive

In the contemporary information society, it requires one to have a particularly isolated and cloistered life not to be in the path of informational torrent. The flood of information numbs the ability of any typical individual to prioritize, let alone be incisive in analysis. Information overload and the conflicting interpretations that emanate with or without expert scrutiny, especially on the Internet, leads to stressful perceptions and dilemmas of "to do or not to do." Yet, some of the information pieces are true nuggets of wisdom (as the cited CNN article). Being alert and attentive helps one cope with the stress of being overtaken by progressively or rapidly changing situations. Being alert means the ability to think quickly and being quick to notice things.

Alertness, equally, enables a person to judge the nuggets for their true worth quickly and develop response plans. Alertness is reinforced by attentiveness. Being attentive means listening or watching something carefully and with interest. Significant stress is generated when people are not attentive and either pass up opportunities (pointers from placement talks by companies, for example) or get into difficulties (not heeding to traffic signage, for example). Typically, all of us get but a few seconds to note each information bit of the information torrent of each day. One needs to be alert and attentive to make the best use of such seconds and the information bytes. At the other pole position, being alert and attentive is the only way to remain safe (protected from danger or harm) and stable (steady and undisturbed) through anticipation and caution, whether one is old or young.

Communicative and Corrective

Unreasonable external environments could sap one's energies and make unreasonable demands on one's ability to cope with pressure, leading to stress. Most of us would have lived with unpardoning teachers or autocratic bosses. The more volatile the external environment, the less resilient one's internal faculties become. This, coupled with the traditional Indian mindset of just taking orders from superiors rather than debating contrarian viewpoints, results in people building up stressful and bottled-up emotions within themselves. As the CNN article says, communication and correction are necessary when the external dependencies warrant it.

One's ability to be effective in communication depends on one's maturity. Maturity is the quality of thinking, expressing, and behaving in a sensible manner. Maturity helps individuals take the adversity in one's stride and look beyond the problems for opportunities. Correction would, in this context, mean self-correction too. The ability of mature communication flows from a strong sense of reasoned self-worth. Respect (and not arrogance) for one's capabilities results in authentic communication. Mature and authentic communication results in better receptivity to correction and has a calming influence on the stress levels. On the other hand, arrogance in one's capabilities leads to abrasive communication which is a trigger for stress build-up.

Primal and Philosophical

Failure is easy to read but success is difficult to fathom. Ironically, people read too much into failure as if it is the end of life and become too smug with success as if it is the proverbial (and automatic) steppingstone to further successes. Both the approaches lead to needless stress levels. Research is a classic example of how failures lead to pioneering successes. Almost all great inventions and discoveries of the past were based on multiple failures of experiments. The exit of leaders and businesses who fail points to the fact that failure is not an option in leadership and business. On the other hand, even success could be a quicksand-like experience; it could result in irrational exuberance that makes one less prepared to confront new challenges and be prone for failures.

Preoccupation with failure and exultation with success are respectively the leading and lagging triggers of stress. The way to cope with the failure–success cycles in life is by being always focused on primal needs. One also needs to be philosophical when the above five factor-pairs: do not yield the anticipated results. Primal denotes certain very basic and fundamental needs that must be always taken care of in life, for oneself and for all those under one's care and protection. Philosophical means having a calm attitude towards a difficult or disappointing situation. This combination of primal–philosophical attributes certainly helps one cope with failures and successes without stress. One who relies on the least possible level of materialism and the most possible level of spirituality enjoys life as no one else would. Unfortunately, only a wise few are blessed to live like that, and hence the need to rely on the paired attribute kit as discussed in this chapter.

Chapter 25

From Procrastination to Decisiveness

Procrastination is the act of putting off or delaying action on something that requires immediate attention and action. Procrastination is often confused with postponement. Both have in their meanings the words "putting off" or "delaying." Postponement is the act of putting off or delaying an originally planned one to a later date. Postponement is relative to a plan and indicates de-prioritization, merited or not. Postponement is often linked to a reluctance to bestow effort, either due to laziness or otherwise. Postponement on certain occasions tends to be benign, and on certain occasions, life-threatening. Postponement at times provides relief, merited or not, to people. Postponement has many times a financial motive; individuals would like to postpone expenses and advance incomes.

Procrastination and postponement are interrelated. Procrastination is postponing something needlessly and mostly indefinitely, without regard to time, effort, resources, or results. Postponement, on the other hand, tends to be tactical opportunism to conserve effort and resources. Both make one lose time, in essence, and delay or totally avoid outcomes or lose results. Procrastination is said to be the thief of time by Benjamin Franklin. Mahatma Gandhi said, "The future depends on what you do today." Procrastination, it is said, is often due to fear of failure. Here again, what Mahatma Gandhi said is relevant: "To do what we fear is the first step to success." Dick Cheney, former Vice President of the USA is reported to have said, "I think I was able to survive five heart attacks because I never postponed going to hospital when something didn't feel right." On certain occasions, postponement provides unanticipated results, like landing on a better job relative to the one in hand. Figure 25.1 explains the difference between postponement and procrastination.

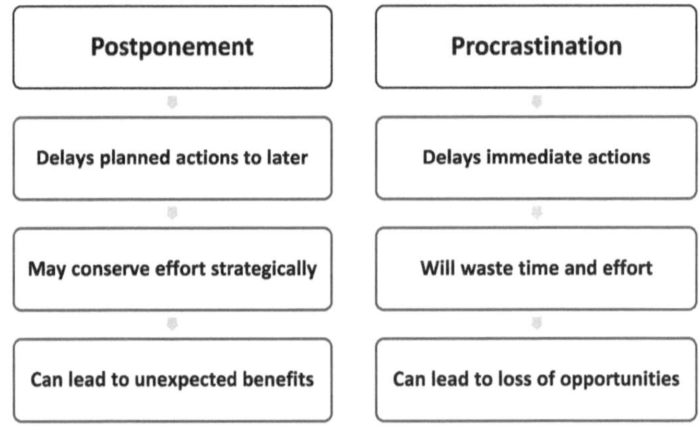

Figure 25.1: Difference between Postponement and Procrastination

Procrastination is Universal

It is imagined that procrastination strikes only certain people who are wired to be procrastinating. The truth is that even apparently productive people tend to procrastinate. People who seem to multitask effortlessly or seem to be putting every idle minute to productive use (for example, working on laptop while waiting in the airport lounge, and also talking on the cell phone) could also be procrastinating on a few vital things. In fact, such visible fury of productive working could be a subtle cover for the ongoing procrastination. Procrastination would well have been left to an individual's choice but for the adverse impact it has on one's own and others' lives.

While occasional procrastination may be inevitable, regular procrastination as a personality trait would have underlying behavioural implications.

There are three principal causes why people succumb to procrastination. At one end of the spectrum, an individual could be so opinionated that he or she is unable to judge the importance of the action he or she must take as well as the rewards of taking the action and the pitfalls of not taking the action. Individuals' approaches to some of the critical lifestyle issues, such as doing proper exercise or taking proper diet, fall into this category. At the other end of the spectrum, an individual could be so obsessed with perfectionism that he or she would never embark on anything for fear of outcomes being not to expectations or receiving criticisms. Most people fall between the two ends of the spectrum, weighed down by a whole range of issues relating to time management, emotional burdening, and mood swings.

Loop of Procrastination

Procrastination is a continuous loop that takes hold of an individual the moment he or she enters the loop once. The usual entry point into the loop is delay in acting on something due to a lack of awareness of its importance, and lack of appreciation of the essence of timeliness. As one avoids acting on the matter, the negative consequences of inaction start becoming apparent, both by comparison and by self-evaluation. A student putting off studies or a software engineer putting off the testing of his code fall into the same category. As the hopelessness caused by the delay becomes evident, the individual slips into a negative mood that could lead to one of the three outcomes: he could entirely give up with total nonchalance or helplessness; he could try to complete it by leaving everything else with total burnout; or do what he can with a low level of self-worth. In any of the routes, the emotional consequences are negative. Figure 25.2 explains the procrastination loop.

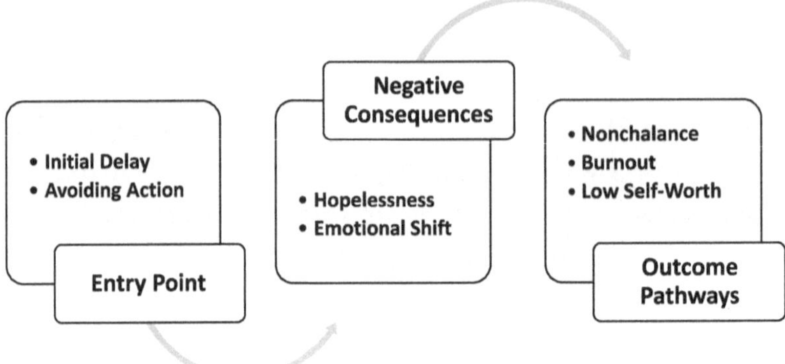

Figure 25.2: The Procrastination Loop

Procrastination, once done on any issue, typically leads to more procrastination, and on more issues. A student who burns midnight oil to cram everything prior to the examination deadline would be leaving out all other extracurricular activities and even may be skipping the day classes. The software engineer who defers testing to the penultimate day may fumble to remediate even small errors. As the negative emotions start taking charge, one would start distancing oneself from peers and others, and avoiding carrying out even daily chores, be it reading a newspaper or checking an email. The feeling of guilt associated with not being oneself only worsens the mood. Depending on the emotional personality of the individual, the feeling of guilt could be manageable or unmanageable. When procrastination starts weighing down on one's life, one must start taking external help for structured approaches to break the loop of procrastination.

Ten Helpful Principles

The following ten principles that are simple in logic but complex in terms of behaviour for an individual to control, overcome, and eliminate procrastination.

1. ***Openness***

   The first step in beating procrastination is being open; open about the required actions and the likely consequences. Openness also includes taking a broader view of life than a myopic view of just one event. For example, starting an exercise regimen should not be seen as an allocation of 30 minutes a day but rather as a component of total lifestyle. One tends to receive inputs all the while through each interaction one has with the external environment, be it people and events. One should be open to receiving the inputs, analysing, and absorbing them, including those that seem to be less critical.

2. ***Reflection***

   The second step in overcoming procrastination is being reflective and introspective; understanding one's own reluctance to apply oneself to the task even though the requirements and consequences are known. One must figure out whether it is a question of time and effort, habit and bias or mood and ambience. Figuring out the reasons for procrastination is the most important step towards conquering procrastination.

3. ***Clearance***

   The third step relates to carefully identifying the obstacles in the path that are related to one's own body, mind, and personal ecosystem. Releasing additional time out of the limited time available, each day, would be the most effective way to overcome the barriers. Uncluttering of one's assets, be it home, desk, or inbox would be one way; in some cases, becoming an early morning person would be the solution, and in some cases being a night owl would be the answer. In all cases, being ahead of the curve in terms of time and effort is the key.

4. ***Dive-in***

   In most cases, the unknown does give trepidation, even to the otherwise accomplished individuals. Learning to ride a bike or drive a car is a simple example. Until one faces the challenge of balancing on two wheels or driving through a crowded street, the first move is necessary to address the concerns squarely. The moment the first step is successful, trepidation leads to relief, and as the steps are repeated relief leads to exhilaration, and exhilaration leads to execution.

5. ***Perseverance***

   Not in all cases dive-ins help; in a few cases there could be failures leading to the deepening of negative emotions and moods. Perseverance backed by an evaluation of what went wrong, and the execution of a remediation plan is the answer. However, it is easier said than implemented. This is one area where help from the immediate environment would be very helpful. Openness to seek help would be important, though.

6. ***Right-Sizing***

   Failure is often related to aspirations being far more than what resources can support. Having more on the plate than what can one chew is one of the primary triggers for procrastination. One would be better off doing a few things right rather than staring blankly at a long laundry list of things to do. Unmanageable projects intimidate any person. As an example, even researchers who are conditioned to be patient in the face of failures eventually discover that a simple pilot experiment or a synopsis of the research project provides greater confidence than trying to execute a mega experiment or script a thesis right away.

7. ***Celebration***

   While activity is never an achievement, celebrating key activities reinforces one's ability to overcome procrastination. As one sets about constructing a huge website, developing a homepage itself deserves a celebration. As one embarks on a start-up, getting the certificate of incorporation itself qualifies for a celebration. Celebrations linked to successes trigger the androgen, serotonin, and norepinephrine receptors in one's brain to elevate one's mood. Positive mood is the most important aid to overcome procrastination. Celebrating results is, of course, the ultimate success in overcoming procrastination.

8. ***Optimization***

   Perfection has a place but not everywhere, every time. Perfection is also contextual. In the early phases of conquering procrastination, perfectionists would need to reappraise their penchant for perfection. There is an insightful quotation in journalism: "You can edit a bad page, but you can't edit a blank page." An optimized result that can be celebrated is worth more than a perfect aspiration that may never see the light of the day.

9. ***Self-Motivation***

   Self-motivation is the last of the final two steps in decisively overcoming procrastination. The ability to forgive oneself for one's failures and motivate oneself for the required success is important in the fight against procrastination. As Mahatma Gandhi said, "thoughts become words, words become behaviours, behaviours become habits, habits become values, and values become destiny". Self-motivation requires self-awareness about one's aptitudes and competencies so that one is motivated by the possibilities of achievement.

10. ***Ecosystem***

    The ultimate support and insurance for eliminating, and even avoiding procrastination, is an ecosystem that supports all the above principles. Having the right friends and right colleagues who operate in an environment of decisiveness, timeliness, and goal orientation is an extremely important determinant. At times, one would need to move to a better environment as a systemic antidote to procrastination.

Time as a Resource

A fundamental driver for overcoming procrastination is an appreciation by the individual of the importance of time as a resource. An idea or activity put off due to procrastination tends to have a snowballing effect. On the other hand, an individual who learns to be timely in his thoughts and actions will learn to be decisive. Being resolute against procrastination is half the battle won; learning to be decisive is the full battle won!

Chapter 26

Hard and Soft Employee Skills

An employee's competency set should comprise both hard skills and soft skills. Hard skills are those that reflect technical and analytical capabilities, whereas soft skills are those that deal with communication and collaboration capabilities. A well-rounded manager should be adept in both hard skills and soft skills. Hard skills, which are technical and professional in nature, are predominantly acquired through education, whereas soft skills are predominantly personality-based and are improved through experience. Trainers typically tend to view these as two distinct streams of learning and development. Hard skills are rarely imparted in organizations except through on-the-job training. Each time an equipment or facility is upgraded, or product and process specifications are revised, the experience of working with the changes teaches the employees new hard skills. On an exceptional basis, employees also are retooled through customized educational programs in universities.

On the other hand, experience that helps the employees upgrade their hard skills ironically very often leads to distortion of soft skills. Employees tend to become somewhat egoistic and rigid (depending on their cultural evolution) as well as authoritative or withdrawn (depending on whether they are extroverted or introverted respectively). Functions become rigid organizations within organizations, with growing inter-functional distances, making communication and collaboration exceedingly difficult, both at functional and individual levels. Given these cultural characteristics, the concentration of organizations tends to be on developing the soft skills of employees on one hand and changing the cultural dynamics of the organization on the other. Trainers and HR managers generally concur that such programs usually have limited impact and fail to bring about fundamental and lasting improvements to employee soft skills or organizational cultural dynamics.

Hard versus Soft; or Hard with Soft?

The distinction between hard skills and soft skills is appropriate but the attempt to treat them as two distinct streams of continuing education is inappropriate. A person's soft skills determine how open he or she is to improve his or her hard skills. Hard skills are not merely skills of engineering or accountancy that are robotically imparted. Significant person-to-person interaction is also required to imbibe new hard skills. A person who is egoistic and rigid is likely to have a closed mind on asking questions and seeking knowledge while a humble and flexible person is likely to be all eager and willing to learn new knowledge. More importantly, hard skills are likely to involve a host of technical and professional disciplines that need to work together to deliver the total systemic effectiveness. A manufacturing engineer, for example, would need to understand how his machine tools operate and fail, and how they are maintained. A maintenance engineer must understand why and how design and manufacturing tolerances are achieved.

Interpersonal communication and collaboration, across technical functions, are vital to optimize the hard-skill learning processes. Equally, soft skills do not exist in vacuum. The soft skills of communication, collaboration, and time management, for example, may be required in teamwork for designing products, conducting operations, managing finances, or developing markets. However, these goals themselves require hard skills. Without hard skills that lead to design creativity, manufacturing excellence, accounting integrity, and market mapping, these hard jobs cannot happen successfully. Possessing mere soft skills cannot lead to the delivery of technical and functional jobs. In addition, several soft skills require a measure of hard skills, be it language skills, computer skills, or presentation skills, for a person to be expressive, efficient, and effective. It goes without further elaboration that hard skills and soft skills are integral to each other, and even symbiotic. Organizations must find holistic paradigms to impart both the kinds of skills amongst the employees simultaneously. Figure 26.1 presents a framework of hard skills and soft skills.

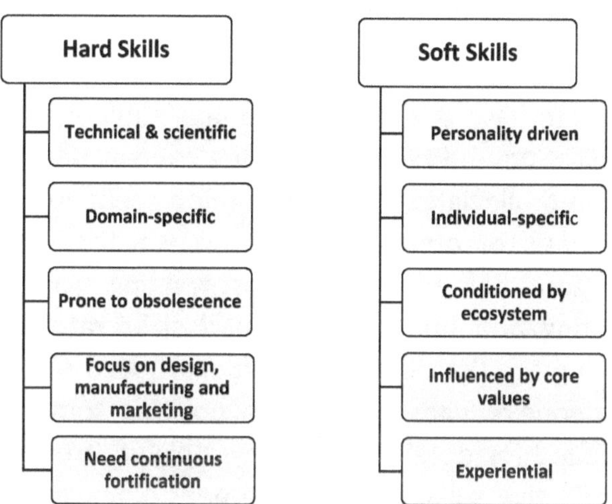

Figure 26.1: A Framework of Hard Skills and Soft Skills

Laying the Foundations

In the Indian educational scenario, the technical and professional educational stream is considered distinct from the language and fine arts educational stream. As one may surmise, the latter stream provides the foundations of soft skills. In technical and professional institutions, language courses are limited probably to just one semester and fine arts courses are virtually non-existent. As a result, students could be technically brilliant but tend to be lagging in terms of soft skills. As a converse phenomenon, arts and language courses have very few technical and professional subjects that could enhance the conceptual and analytical capabilities of a student. This differentiation is further accentuated by the fact that from the school-going stage itself, school children and their parents tend to zero in on preferred careers and accordingly focus on the related subjects, and defocus on what they consider to be unrelated subjects. The foundations of basic education thus tend to be less than holistic, even if they are specialty oriented.

Efforts by certain higher technological institutions such as the IITs to have one or two language subjects or business communication and technical writing courses hardly provide the required alleviation. Even in the job scenario, given that the emphasis of organizations is on achieving immediate delivery from their employees, most training programs focus on adapting and updating the hard skills rather than on overcoming the deficiencies of soft skills. As a result, by the time someone reaches a managerial position, some of the soft skills needed for obtaining effective delivery from others or having effective collaboration with peer managers would be found to be missing, impacting organizational performance.

Although organizations mount soft skills programs for middle-level and senior-level managers, such attempts would often be a case of "too little, and too late." The problem is also accentuated by the "ego hurt" seniors feel when they are expected to develop their soft skills at a late stage, and the consequent defensive as well as aggressive reactions, making the desired culture of collaborative delivery even more elusive in an organization. Another negative consequence of this distinction is that technical specialists tend to be confined to line functions, whereas non-technical people gravitate towards staff functions, making holistic leadership development to meet the requirements of apex positions even more challenging.

Easy to Lose, Difficult to Acquire

The hard skills and soft skills are correlated with learning and development. Hard skills are acquired in a relatively well-structured manner through the educational system but are easy to lose. As employees become accustomed to operating in established technological systems of firms, the gap between emerging technologies and established technologies widens, leading to knowledge obsolescence. As employees move up the hierarchy, ecosystems, and management processes distance the employees from their machines, because of which they lose their hard skills relatively easily. My observation is that employees tend to be technologically and professionally contemporary in the first one-third of their career span, and thereafter experience a decline in their hard skills. The hard skills are easy to lose for employees who do not make special efforts to update themselves. There can be no permanence at all in hard skills, and updating hard skills is indeed a challenging task, especially given the strides in digital and disruptive technologies such as artificial intelligence.

As certain organizations and certain employees emphasize soft skills to a greater degree, hard skills become easier to lose. In contrast, soft skills are more difficult to acquire but once acquired tend to be more difficult to lose. Soft skills are acquired not merely through the educational stream but more importantly through life experience itself. The propensity to acquire certain, if not all, soft skills is very much a personality-related matter, and in a sense tends to be a genetically influenced factor too. Depending on the congeniality levels that existed in family, school, and college environments, a person could be positioned in terms of propensity to absorb soft skills. Interpersonal skills are experiential and once acquired remain embedded. While one does come across instances of aggressive people mellowing or self-effacing people becoming more emphatic over a lifetime, basic changes in personality disposition are difficult to come by. While language skills may be easy to acquire equally by diverse people, the way communication is conceptualized and delivered by each person would continue to be personality specific. While people may be trained to adopt a particular style of interpersonal relationship, often, adopted behaviours tend to wilt and natural behaviours are likely to surface under stressful circumstances.

C-Suite Requirements

Figure 26.2 presents a leadership skill grid based on the relative mix of hard skills and soft skills in a leader or a manager. The way hard skills and soft skills are taught in educational institutions, the way they are imparted by family and social ecosystems, and the processes by which they are updated by on-the-job experiences ironically run counter to the need to develop holistic business or corporate leadership. Like several of the managerial templates, the managerial grid advocating that leaders should have more of strategic skills (or soft skills) and less of technical skills (or hard skills) at the leadership level is a deficient model. A music conductor, however eminent, cannot afford to forget how the musical notes are written. A surgeon, the more eminent he is, the more skilful, technologically updated, and behaviourally competent he must be. The requirements of the corporate C suite are no different and require holistic leaders who are technologically as well as behaviourally competent. The concept that with experience and hierarchical progression, the typical executive can afford to lose the hard skills and needs to be adept only at soft skills is ill-placed.

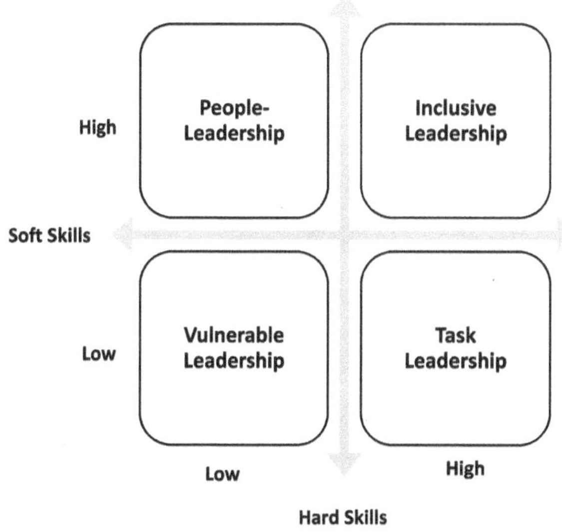

Figure 26.2: Leadership Skill Grid

The C-suite leader, the CXO of whatever domain or the CEO himself or herself, must keep the technical and professional competencies as strong and as updated they had been at the beginning of the career. They must also have an appreciation of what both hard and soft skills can do to enhance the leadership strength. The educational approaches and the experiential strategies that make the hard skills easy to lose and soft skills difficult to acquire need a complete redefinition. If these development models are retuned to develop holistic students, holistic executives, and holistic managers who are high on both hard skills and soft skills, we would have a C-suite bench that is far larger and richer than what India Inc has at present. The enriched C-suite would be a great leading factor in India's quest for globalization. There would be a greater all-round entrepreneurial and big business development in the country and a greater emergence of Indian multinational corporations across the globe. Indian executives, managers, and leaders who are strong on either of hard skills or soft skills must appreciate the need to become equally strong on both the dimensions.

Chapter 27

Conscientious Competence

Several companies globally (Enron, Tyco, WorldCom, and Xerox of the West and Satyam, Kingfisher, and Sahara of the East) had fallen from grace over the last few decades due to mismanagement. Each case is an example of how just one or two top-ranking leaders of a company could cause and perpetuate gross strategic, operational, and financial mistakes of high magnitude reported in each case. The occurrence of such events in a public listed company is even more surprising given the size and scale of operations a large company has, the public visibility it receives, and the innumerable transactions it has with thousands of its stakeholders. The increasing number of audit firms resigning from their audit assignments in India for reasons of management opaqueness is also indicative of some deep-rooted malaise. One conclusion that emerges from such case studies, when one delves deep into them, is that such adverse outcomes cannot be attributed to just one leader, however powerful he or she is in an organization but probably are the result of several individuals working collectively together, knowingly or unknowingly, towards such outcomes.

It is also a resultant of not having enough checks and balances in the system and the Boards being passive in their role. However, even this conclusion is paradoxical in the context of such organizations being expected to have people with established backgrounds and appropriate perspectives. Are these adverse outcomes caused by an organizational behaviour dynamic that is not adequately researched? The answer probably lies in the interplay between two critical dimensions that drive human behaviour. Competence and conscientiousness are the two dimensions that drive the behaviour of any personality, in an organizational context. Competence is the important skill (or skill set) that is needed to do a job effectively. Such competencies are acquired through education and experience. Conscientiousness is the part of an individual's thought process that judges the morality of the individual's own actions. It acts like an ethical compass for the individual, guiding him on the rights and wrongs of actions in an organization. Figure 27.1 presents the drivers of competence and conscientiousness.

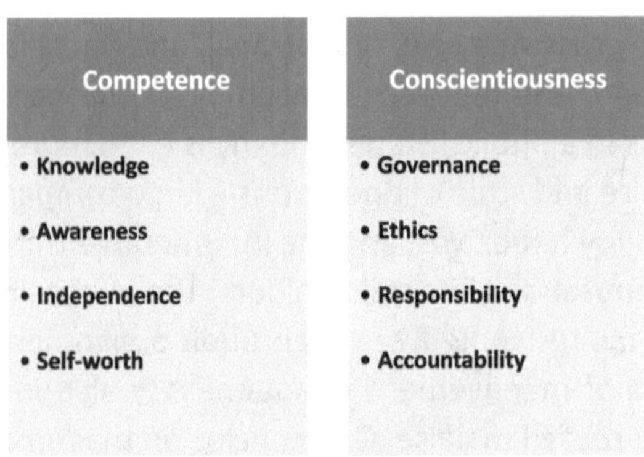

Figure 27.1: Drivers of Competence and Conscientiousness

Competence and Conscientiousness

Competence stems from knowledge and awareness. The more competent a person, the more likely the person is likely to be able to contribute in his or her role to the organization. A competent person is likely to be aware of the various decisions he takes and the implications for business growth and propriety. More importantly, competence provides a unique sense of self-worth and the requisite confidence to an individual to operate in line with the fair dictates of his or her profession. A competent person is thus likely to stand his ground against any undue pressures and conduct his activities in a performance-oriented and ethical manner.

As a corollary, an incompetent person is likely to be a pliant individual susceptible to various types of pressures besides being a poor contributor to corporate performance. Conscientiousness provides the sense of right or wrong to an individual. It helps a person with the requisite sensitivity to analyse whether the decisions and actions he takes by himself or is asked to take by his superiors are consistent with professional and business ethics and practices of good governance. A conscientious person is more likely to exercise his competence in a positive manner for the good of the business and society. As a corollary, a person who is not conscientious is likely to be more amenable to undue pressures and questionable ways, and worse still may even put his competence to misuse in pursuit of short-run gains.

Competence and Conscientiousness Grid

A person's contribution to, and influence over, the ethical performance of a company is thus an interplay of these two essential dimensions of a personality. The issues one encounters in various organizations are linked to the variability that is found in each of these the two dimensions. Like every attribute or outcome in the universe, competence and conscientiousness also follow stochastic distributions. In a well-run organization, the talent pool is likely to reflect a normal distribution in terms of levels of competence and conscientiousness each. This implies that a very large number of people would be reasonably competent and conscientious while a small percentage at either end would be either highly incompetent and non-conscientious or extraordinarily competent and conscientious.

One can, therefore, view the human resource base of an organization, irrespective of the domain specialization or the hierarchy level to which the talent pool belongs, in terms of a 2×2 matrix that classifies people in terms of high or low levels of competency or conscientiousness. Organizations being the sum of individual profiles, the aggregation of competency–conscientiousness profiles of the individuals also contribute to the organizational DNA. An interplay of these two dimensions of a collective human resource base results in organizations that are clearly differentiated, as shown by the 2×2 organizational grid below and illustrated in Figure 27.2.

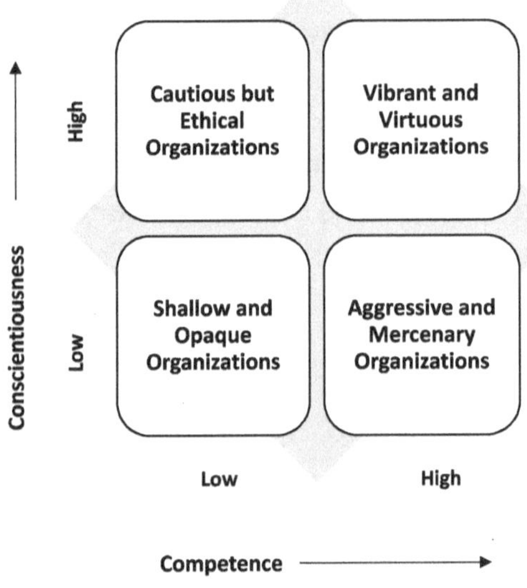

High in competence and High in conscientiousness: Vibrant and Virtuous organizations
High in competence and Low in conscientiousness: Aggressive and Mercenary organizations
Low in competence and High in conscientiousness: Static but Ethical organizations
Low in competence and Low in conscientiousness: Shallow and Opaque organizations

Figure 27.2: Competence–Conscientiousness Grid

Organizations that have people with high levels of individual competence and conscientiousness turn out to be vibrant and virtuous organizations and demonstrate industry-leading performance in business, ethics, innovation, quality, governance, and safety. These firms figure consistently as the top rankers in the blue chip league and often set the tone in all aspects of corporate behaviour. Companies such as Toyota fall in this category. Organizations that have large pools of highly competent people but with low levels of conscientiousness typically post high business growth rates. However, the methods they deploy to achieve the performance could be questionable. These organizations are typically driven overwhelmingly by a performance criterion and are likely to choose the quantitative goals of performance over qualitative ideals of ethics, governance, or safety if it were to come to a crunch ever. They are seen as aggressive and mercenary organizations.

Typical performance-obsessed companies that are loved by investors with a short-term perspective for the momentum of their earnings fall in this category. Organizations that have a preponderance of people who subscribe to high levels of ethics but have not bothered to equip themselves with the competencies required to handle the challenges of modern-day business would be virtuous organizations but with pedestrian performance. Though such organizations have the ability and intent to do good to the economy and the society, they would be unable to do so for want of requisite technical and managerial bandwidth. Many traditional, value-based family-held businesses and NGOs run by individual champions fall in this category. Organizations that are low in competence and conscientiousness are a drag to the economy as well as society, for they represent a waste of public resources.

In addition, if these companies desire to emulate high-performance companies without the inherent competence and conscientiousness, they could pose a grave risk to the economy and society. Such companies could resort to questionable means to grow in business. Short-term tactics deployed by such companies under the cover of opaque management processes result in hollow and risky business models that are susceptible to collapse at the first downturn. From Enron to Satyam, gigantic corporate failures took place in companies with such low levels of competence–conscientiousness mix that fail to support the aspirations of high achievement.

Leadership Responsibility

Given the interplay discussed above, the top leadership in an organization must aim at enlarging the human resource pool that is truly both competent and conscientious while correcting, failing which eliminating, the human resource base that is patently low in competence and conscientiousness. Efforts also should focus on the other two grids that require increase in competence and conscientiousness as required so that the virtuous grid is maximized. This is easier said than done for a couple of reasons. Competence is often measurable and visible as quantitative outcomes of performance, whereas conscientiousness is a matter of qualitative perception. It is a matter of further complication that a high level of quantitative performance could itself be due to low levels of conscientiousness.

Organizations must deploy 360-degree analysis during the recruitment, training, and performance appraisal phases of their HRM so that everyone is analysed in terms of not only the individual's competence and conscientiousness levels but also how he or she integrates these two essential factors in terms of a performance work ethic. The top leadership of a company must necessarily set the pace for processes that recognize and reward individuals only when their competencies are combined with conscientiousness. Such an approach will doubtless help create an organizational DNA that is virtuous and vibrant, leading to high performance with high ethics.

Chapter 28

Rational and Emotional

Technology evolves so rapidly that many conventional living tools and processes seem redundant from time to time. We are in an age where computers have reduced the effort of human thinking, and algorithms have taken over the art of decision-making. The future is one of Artificial Intelligence which could make many conventional activities redundant. Many of the human faculties—which in earlier generations used to be developed through challenged human effort from childhood—have been automated through a plethora of electronic devices. A whole new generation has grown up with Google that answers every question through an instantaneous web of information and with Facebook as well as other social media sites that connect millions in a borderless global society. The new generations will find generative and conversational artificial intelligence making a marked difference to human thought and action processes.

The world is moving into a counterintuitive phase where higher levels of technology that require greater levels of skill are also rendering larger numbers of people less skilful. Several decades ago, at a very basic level, slide rules were replaced by calculators and calculators by computers in engineering education; memory switches in the brain have been replaced by mere taps of fingers for Web searches. From pilotless aircraft to driverless cars, and from synthetic music to combinatorial chemistry, the future of automation, replacing human effort and ingenuity, is clear. The relentless progress of science and technology is, without notice and awareness, creating an intellectual skew. While a few elite educational and research institutions will keep developing experts who can innovate such controlling technologies, the broader universe of educational institutions are likely to churn out multitudes of professionals who are induced to subordinate conventional braininess to the more convenient electronic guidance. Increasing technological intensity also makes individuals introverted and impersonal, depriving them of social skills.

The technological trends and educational practices raise serious questions. Will the next-generation professional be any longer an original thinker or independent doer? Addicted as he or she is to smart devices and virtual networks, would the professional of the future be able to connect with the society as the previous generation professionals were? Do we need to consciously reinvent the process of professionalization to restore the human element of an increasingly overwhelming techno-economic system? Will the new generation focus only on economic prosperity to the detriment of social equity? The answer lies in re-educating the new generation through a mix of rational and emotional skills.

Rational and Emotional Skills

As long as the society remains an agglomeration of human beings, and not robots and not even humanoids, a human being has a great responsibility to retain the essential skills that characterize the fundamental human capabilities. From a viewpoint of an economic society or a business organization, from the plethora of human capabilities and attributes, a prioritized set of rational and emotional skills can be identified that must be nurtured through generations. As illustrated in figure 28.1, the five rational skills are optimal reading, manual writing, mental calculation, extended memory, and physical artistry. The five emotional skills are dynamic self-worth, collaborative competition, respectful independence, ethical compliance, and social trusteeship.

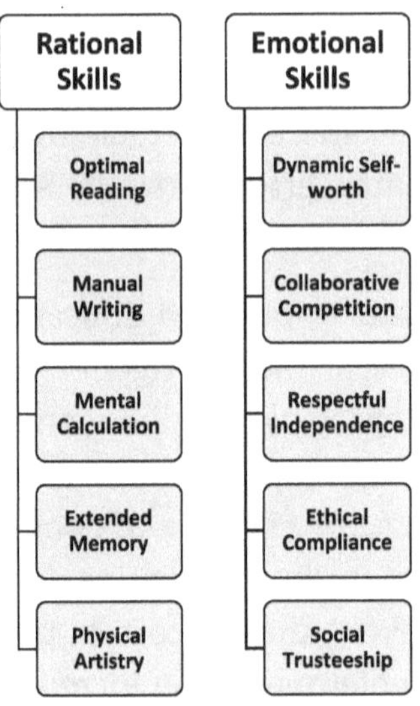

Figure 28.1: Rational and Emotional Skills

The rational skills are so named because of the need to steer the learning generation, through conscious efforts, away from the growing dependence of the mind on the Internet to rediscovery of original thinking and natural performance. The emotional skills are so named because of the need to combine the very many emotions a human being has into synergistic combinations that enhance human personality and social relatedness. These ten rational and emotional skills ensure that the current and future generations regain their intuitive and intrinsic ability for (i) multi-faculty development, (ii) synchronization of the mind and the limbs, (iii) alignment of the head and the heart, (iv) complementing of the gut and the soul, and (v) harmonization of the individual and the society.

Developing and using these skills will ensure that technology makes life lively. Science, technology, and business will have the humanization theme as the core of development. Every turn of technological development must be used to reinforce these rational and emotional skills.

Rational Skill Development

The hypothesis of this chapter may be counter to the beliefs of the new techno-generation, which believes that simplification, virtualization, and even elimination of established practices is inevitable and irreversible. The reality, however, is that such technology buffs are losing their mental and intellectual acumen because of their dependence on electronic gadgets and software tools. Without attempting to reverse the technological evolution, we can combine new technologies and past practices to enhance the intellectual capabilities overall. Mercifully, the technological evolution is so diverse that the essentials of life and living, seen to be under extinction, come back to life, albeit reinvented with greater sophistication. As discussed below, this exciting nature of the technological evolution is the core of human skill development too.

1. ***Optimal Reading***

   As the famous quotes on books suggest books are among the greatest companions one can have. That said, books, like friends, must be well chosen. Good books serve as companions across generations. Digitization of print and writing, and the emergence of electronic readers have placed in our hands unimaginable bytes of reading material. The new generation must, however, learn to be discerning and focused even as it is enabled to be diversified and unbounded in its quest for knowledge. Digital libraries are a highly portable boon and can be effectively used to scan the world of writings. However, every reader must have his or her own physical bookshelf that stores for him or her the "well-chosen books of all time." An optimal mix of digital and physical book reading keeps a person better informed and better equipped.

2. ***Manual Writing***

   With the ubiquitous growth of the personal and laptop computers and their typewriting-style keyboards, it looked as if the new generations would be completely oblivious of handwriting. For those generations of teachers and the taught that started their education on slate and chalk, the keyboard threatened to be the greatest disconnect with the fundamentals of learning. With tablets, phablets and stylus pens (thank Apple and Samsung, once again) coming onto the centre stage vigorously, a human hand and an electronic slate can coexist harmoniously, and even productively. Manual writing provides for the free flow of thought and the calibrated conversion of thoughts into letters. The beauty and the orderliness with which one's letters are formed constitute the positive reflections of one's personality. Unlike the rigidity of keyboard typing, the flexibility of handwritten scribbles is often the fountainhead of spontaneous creativity. One should never lose the touch and feel of manual writing to be able to stay innovative.

3. ***Mental Calculation***

   Ever since the discovery of numbers took place, human life became dependent on the mastery of numbers. Such mastery has two components: an ability to form the numbers, and an ability to interpret numbers. Calculative abilities in the past distinguished one over the other in sizing up and scaling up challenges and opportunities. With the advent of calculators, people lost the ability to make quick mental calculations. The adverse impact of this sadly goes beyond the obvious; it impacts the spatial ability of a person. While there may be no educational need in today's world to practice multiplications and divisions of double-digit numbers, a grip on number manipulation and computation provides a significant strength to tactical transaction and strategic investment perspectives of social and economic life.

4. ***Extended Memory***

Open book examinations and multiple-choice questions have served to reduce mindless cramming and to make solution development a guided activity for students. However, technology has taken over the minds of people, making the human race virtually memory averse. This is a great risk for human genetics and the evolution of the intellectual part of the DNA. Today's student or citizen has ceased to memorize and is instead tempted to "google" (and now to ask ChatGPT) for any information. It is the Cloud that feeds instant information and solutions to any and all questions and problems. Considering that the human brain has an enormous capability to store and process data, the addiction and resort to search engines on the web rather than the processing capabilities in the brain is quite capable of causing atrophy of key mental faculties. We should encourage ourselves to memorize in competition to Google, using the search engine to extend our memory to digital depths and expanses previously not capable of being handled. As one googles by habit as well as temptation, it pays to recreate questions, interrelate answers, and acquire scan-and-store memorizing capabilities.

5. ***Physical Artistry***

   Many things may change in life with technology, but physical activity and artistic expression tend to be fundamentally unchanged at the core. Sports and arts are the best expressions of learning effort and execution perfection. They signify the core of the mind–body coordination that can provide unchanged levels of physical and mental challenge. As a corollary, sports and arts are best suited to restore the eroding capabilities of the human race. Extra-curricular activities in academic and business settings will go a long way in enabling a human being function at his or her maximal capabilities. The strength of public performance, which tests the limits of physical and mental endurance, is often a great influence on the performers as well as the spectators. Activity and artistry come naturally to human life; the new generation should get over synthetic technology and sedentary living to realize the natural potential of hard sports and fine arts.

Emotional Skill Development

If rational skills enable performance at a fundamental level, emotional skills accentuate or attenuate performance. Performance often takes place in a team setting, within a company, an industry, a country, and even globally. An ability to relate oneself to the individual and group dynamics, and in a broader sense to the larger society, is essential to complement rational skills. However, singular emotions are less relevant than specific combinations of emotions if the rational skills are to be meaningfully reinforced. A conceptual framework of emotional skills is presented below.

1. ***Dynamic Self-Worth***

   Every human being has some worth as every activity he or she is capable of performing has some value. It is important for individuals, therefore, to be constructively aware of the value they can bring to the table. The greater the rational skill level one has, the greater will be the value that one can bring to one's organization. The greater the extent to which one is self-reliant, the greater is also the worth that one has. A heightened awareness of self-worth on the part of each team member is essential for healthy team dynamics. At the same time, the concept of self-worth has to be tested dynamically with the changing needs and contemporary skill availability. If a person fails to update skills in dynamic equilibrium with the environment, self-worth that was justifiable at an earlier point of time would simply become an egoistic state of mind.

2. ***Collaborative Competition***

   A techno-savvy generation tends be confident of its ability to manage challenges through technology. A high level of skill inventory is desirable but not always possible. This applies to individuals as much as to organizations or corporations. Individuals and companies that place excessive emphasis on self-reliance and are aggressive in competing with all the other players for both resources and markets are likely to be uncompetitive in the end. An ability to leverage on each other's skills and assets helps individuals and corporations to optimize on costs and efforts. The ability of Sony and Samsung to collaborate on flat panels helped both organizations enhance scale and competitiveness. Automobile makers and component makers have succeeded in continuous product value addition through working as competitive partners rather than wielders of buyer or supplier power. This happened because leaders, managers and executives in such companies became collaboration-oriented in the design and manufacturing space while being competitive in the marketplace. Organizations, whether for-profit or not-for-profit, can collaborate for greater economic and social synergy. An ability to collaborate with apparently competing or contesting team members, departments, or domains requires high strategic maturity.

3. ***Respectful Independence***

   The new generation is independent, emotionally and economically. Even in countries that traditionally believed in the joint family system, proximity rather than togetherness seems to be gaining ground. Certain advanced countries that inculcate independence from the very early years probably promote a culture of independence far too aggressively. Such a culture could potentially fail to take advantage of the wisdom that comes with experience and the maturity that comes with age. Generational gaps have been a reality of human evolution, with each successive generation believing that it knew better than the previous generation. History, however, is replete with examples of how heeding to seasoned advice would have led to more favourable outcomes. Regardless of the integration of such cultural hues in the family and educational systems, professionals should make special efforts to balance the urge for independence with the desirability of gaining from the seasoned and experienced seniors.

4. ***Ethical Compliance***

Ethics differentiate a true professional from an opportunistic player. Ethics are easy to espouse but hard to live by. Ethical compliance comes from a value system that is ingrained deep within the psyche of each individual. Lasting recognition follows ethical compliance. Ethical compliance often demands sacrifices that go beyond the call of normal work and a level of transparency that builds trust all around. Mahatma Gandhi epitomized ethical living through and for a noble cause, beyond compare. There would be opportunities in each person's personal and professional lives to demonstrate how one can be a role model for others by displaying diligence and dutifulness, candour, and collaboration, as well as concern and caring. The ethical compass of a leader or a manager as an individual sets the ethical direction and standard for his or her company.

5. ***Social Trusteeship***

Pursuit of materialism is a concomitant of economic capitalism. As economic affluence grows and purchasing power increases, the new generation understands the success of prosperity rather than the tribulations of poverty. On the other hand, professionals have an important role in influencing how wealth is generated and deployed for the good of the society. These extend from the choice of product lines, business spaces, product development, and manufacturing efficiencies to customer service and corporate social responsibility. The new generation should utilize science and technology to develop products and services for the bottom of the social pyramid. Start-ups and firms with entrepreneurial thinking can take the lead in deploying science and technology for social trusteeship.

NextGen: Skill Matrix

Human life is paradoxical. Individuals and organizations need to score over other individuals and organizations, respectively, to remain competitive and generate wealth. Yet, one must live for, and with, others to lend equity and stability to the social and economic systems. Both the objectives are essential and complementary. The former needs rational skills and the latter emotional skills. As the new generation raises immersed in new technologies, it is likely that the millennials miss out on their intrinsic physical–mental faculties and human relationship skills. As illustrated in Figure 28.2, only by committing to combine rational skills with emotional skills, the new generation can make the society a better place.

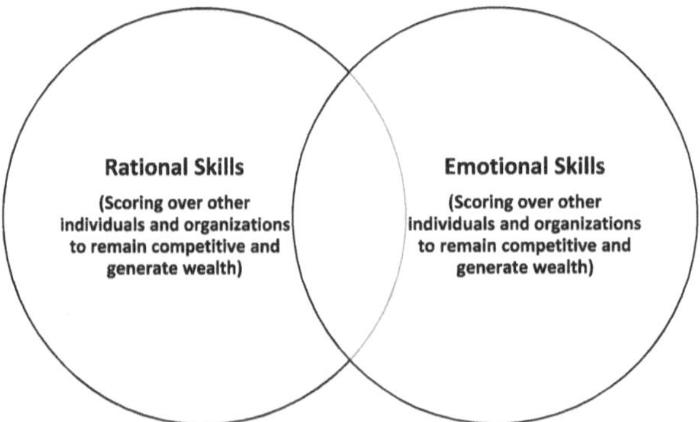

Figure 28.2: Combining Rational Skills with Emotional Skills

Chapter 29

Responsible Communication

One of the critical aspects of personal mastery is control over the words we speak and write. Words have enormous power, more enormous than one tends to understand these days. The ability to express through the written and spoken word is the most important characteristic that differentiates human beings from all other known living creatures. Scientists hypothesize that the development of complex language was a key to the evolution and advancement of humanity. From the spoken word to the written word, it has been a most influential and most dynamic discovery of human memory. Civilizations and cultures were preserved by the words as spoken, and more importantly as written. Yet, words do good as well as bad, and some people even tend to dismiss the impact saying, "these are just words." Equally, societies become fragmented between speakers and listeners, and between writers and readers.

Words are the most important constituent of social relationships and business contracts. A whole range of vows and promises as well as agreements and contracts are expressed through words, and solely words. The traditional societies accord great importance to the spoken word as a contract that must be honoured in letter and spirit. The developed societies lay great store in capturing the intent, execution, and consequences in terms of long and complex legal contracts. While there was law and order as a function from times immemorial, there is no evidence that the written word was vested with so much legal import as it is vested with now. One would, therefore, imagine that words are more important than ever. Unfortunately, however, the more legal the words became, the more travesty of justice began to be encountered in modern societies. Figure 29.1 brings out the three important worthy facets of words.

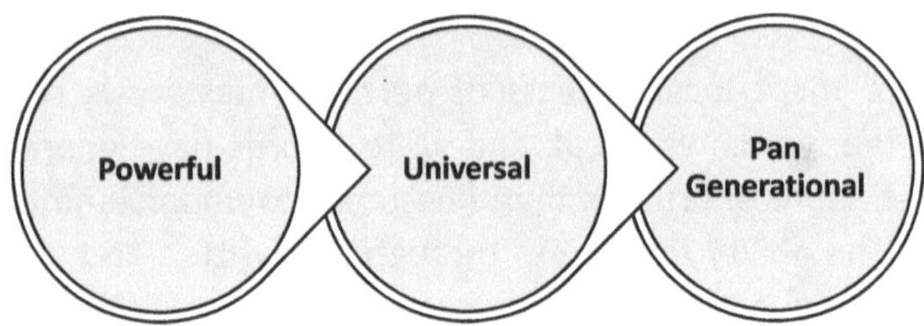

Figure 29.1: The Worth of Words

Word Quotes

Words are so powerful that some become timeless quotes, retaining their power and relevance across generations. The great epics of various religions paint a rich tapestry of teachings. Hinduism probably has the world's most extensive heritage of impactful words expressed through vedas, upanishads, epics, keertanas, mythologies, and theologies. In contemporary English, an anonymous writer has said so effectively: "Watch your thoughts; they become your words. Watch your words; they become your actions. Watch your actions; they become your habits. Watch your habits; they become your character. And watch your character; it becomes your destiny." Societies, doubtless, are shaped by words, and words alone. Words by themselves are not worth the meaning unless backed by actions. Benjamin Franklin observed, "Words may show a man's wit, but actions his meaning." Thoughts, without words serve no purpose, and words without action have little credibility.

Words become more powerful when they are delivered with passion, piety, and authenticity. Words become more powerful also when they are backed by actions. Swami Vivekananda, the great spiritual leader of India was known for his crystal-clear thinking and power-packed delivery. His words "Arise, awake, and stop not till you achieve your goal" are some of the most stirring words ever uttered by a leader. Mahatma Gandhi, the Father of India's Independence, was known for his endearingly simple thinking but he imbued the words with great power by postulating and following nonviolence and satyagraha. It is remarkable that great leaders were devoted to human service, committed to remove inequalities and dedicated to promoting holistic and inclusive living. Though different leaders have different calls of destiny, Mahatma Gandhi was the quintessential charismatic leader who influenced a whole nation with his thoughts, words, and deeds in the chosen goal of national independence.

Word Deluge

Modern world is overwhelmed by a deluge of words. Digital technologies have literally amplified the deluge, with the unbelievable expansion of social media. Legal concerns have made words the addictive stimulants as well as fallacious solutions for a wide range of issues that never bothered the earlier generations. The romantic whiffs and emotional tethers of the past generations are now replaced by broken messages that are punctuated more by smileys, emoticons, and emojis rather than by wit and sincerity. The gentleman's understandings in business are now replaced by long essays of constraints and consequences that are incorporated more for form than for substance. As a result, social relationships as well as business collaborations have become more complex, less utilitarian, and finally more enigmatic. With so many meanings imputed to words, they lose their meaning. And, when words lose meaning, life loses its essence.

When the society is faced with a deluge of words, there tends to be more promise than performance. This is not necessarily due to any bad intentions, per se. Promises require just words while actions require dedication, resources, and efforts. The huge gaps one sees between social aspirations and promises on one hand and tangible goals and visible outcomes on the other can be attributed to people not being thoughtful about promises and circumspect about resources. When business becomes concerned about eventualities, there tends to be more unease of doing business than ease of doing business. This is not due to escapism at any rate. Eventualities require just plans that are tempting to make, whereas outcomes require prioritization, focus, and execution. The huge gaps one sees between business visions and aspirations on one hand and tangible transformations and accomplishments on the other can be attributed to businessmen being carried away by their visions and aspirations with less attention to resource generation and organizational mobilization.

Life's Essence

Life's essence is development. Development requires collaboration. Collaboration is enabled by trust. Trust is reinforced by credibility. Credibility is a result of promise being in line with potential and performance being in line with promise. To complete the loop, authentic promises must be delivered by purposive action. It is, therefore, necessary that one must respect words one uses for their implicit meaning and endeavour to speak what is necessary, commit what is possible, and deliver what is committed. This could be as simple as returning social visits or fulfilling social commitments. In fact, enduring social relationships are built when families, communities, and societies stay together and support each other. The traditional old world is built around the cared and the caretakers living together and families being joint rather than fractured. When economic development and social diffusion throw people asunder, what can still retain the bonding is the power of words on staying committed for each other. Figure 29.2 schematically brings out how meaningful words can drive development.

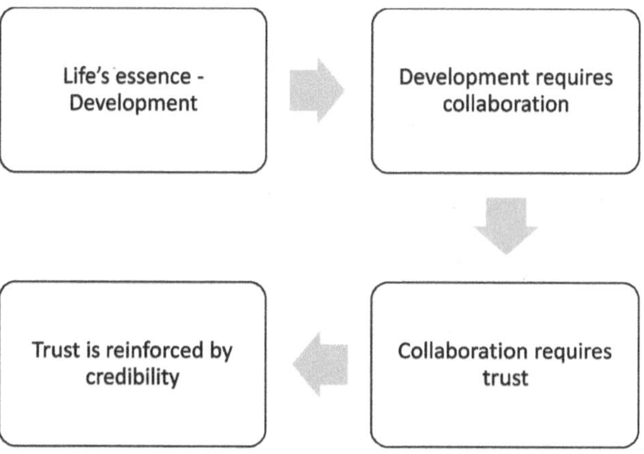

Figure 29.2: Words at the Root of Development

Development's enabler is economic activity. Economic activity requires judicious and productive deployment of resources. Today, a few leading global companies have market capitalization greater than the GDPs of certain nations. This wealth must create more development and must improve the conditions of more people. Those who can help must have both the intent and the platform to help the needy. To enable this, the ease of carrying out economic activity is a must. A start-up cannot fly off immediately if the portal of the Ministry of Corporate Affairs (MCA) does not function for weeks. That the portal was being developed by India's iconic IT bellwether whose new leadership committed itself to artificial intelligence and the like, and that such prolonged glitches did impact the exhortation on the ease of doing business do imply that words are tending to have less meaning in modern business. A modern-day business contract tends to have two pages of deliverables and twenty pages of warranties, assignments, terminations, and consequences. All of these are signed off without the signing authorities not really delving deep into the need for, and implications of, such conditions, and without due discussions on such terms.

Gift of the Gab, Curse of Progress

With words, and their proliferation, the ability to communicate has become a competitive strength for leaders. From intemperate filibuster to suave oratory, the ability to communicate is dictating the course of companies, governments, societies, and nations. The gift of the gab—an ability and aptitude to speak fluently, glibly, and persuasively—has become the hallmark of successful leadership. This was not so in earlier decades wherein words were invariably backed by deeds. Swami Vivekananda's oratory was based on deep spiritual knowledge and with ascetic-like renunciation of pleasures for the uplift of the downtrodden. Mahatma Gandhi's preaching was based on selfless practice of "satyagraha" and nonviolence that could galvanize a nation for inclusive, equitable, and independent life. Such leaders may have had the gift of the gab, but they did not need one, because their thoughts and words were backed by actions and outcomes. With words, and their proliferation, the ability to communicate has become a competitive strength for leaders.

Individuals must develop mastery over language. But that mastery should be accompanied by responsible intent and authentic communication. When words are spoken with an eye on carrying the day, the gift of the gab verily becomes a distraction for the society. Such approach feeds the listeners with grand expectations with little to show on the ground. When companies hire people with extravagant promises, when businesses seek finances with magical returns, when foundations are laid without marshalling resources, and when collaborations are struck with self-serving agendas, the economic ecosystems become exploitative and stress prone. Regimented economies as well as democratic countries have been unable to make meaningful progress when economic arrangements and business contracts are made more in letter and less in spirit.

From social relationships to business contracts, the words must have meanings that are reflected in actions; otherwise, life itself would have little essence. Gautama Buddha said, *"However many holy words you read, However many you speak, What good will they do you, If you do not act upon them?"* There can be no better insight on the importance of words than this!

Chapter 30

Joy of Success

Life is unpredictable in terms of the opportunities and challenges it brings in one's life. Individual life is a part of a family life, and a part of an organizational life. Such an organization could be anything: the genetic family life, informal friends' circle, an executive teams are all organizations. Being successful and happy as a part of the internal family organization and external professional organization is the key objective of every practical person. This chapter explores what could make a person successful and happy in organizations. In doing so, it does not consider the nexus between professional and family success and happiness; nor does it consider one outcome as the trigger of the other. This chapter proposes that both the aspects of life—family and professional—are interrelated and can be optimized for achieving superior success and performance, provided certain basic triggers and drivers of success and happiness in life are understood. However, given that the formal professional organization is an established form of organization that runs on certain principles, such an organization, and an individual in the organization, is taken up to explore the agenda of success and happiness in life.

Success and Happiness

Success and happiness are highly contextual and individualistic, defying easy and common definition. Not all successful people are happy people and not all happy people are successful ones. Success is a materialistic happening and happiness is a philosophical experience, neither being wholly true. Success occurs within and as a result of certain consensual acknowledgement in an organizational system while happiness springs from within the individual, either being only partially true. Success is a measurable and visible metric while happiness is an immeasurable, embedded but experiential emotion; neither is unassailable. This is because metrics and measurements may be wrong as much as smiles and symbolism may be faked. Success takes time to build and could be sustainable or unsustainable (based on strategic effectiveness) while happiness could be ephemeral and transient (and unrelated to successes or failures).

Clearly, there are gross and subtle definitions of success and happiness. As there are no easy and universal definitions of success and happiness, a few baseline criteria would be relevant, combining the context and the individual as well as the organization. Success is often based on accomplishment against a set of organizational and individual goals, in a manner that they are visible and measurable. Success is materialistic to the extent of building value for the organization and an influencing career for the individual. Happiness is a sense of fulfilment that a person or a group of persons experiences when the person or the group receives economic or non-economic recognition, directly or indirectly linked to the person's or the group's contributions. Happiness is individualistic, and is both materialistic and philosophical, to the extent that depending on the philosophical and emotional disposition of an individual, he or she may choose to accentuate or attenuate the happiness quotient. Be that as it may, it is important for individuals in an organization to understand the means of deriving and sustaining success as well as happiness. Figure 30.1 illustrates the Characteristics of Success and Happiness.

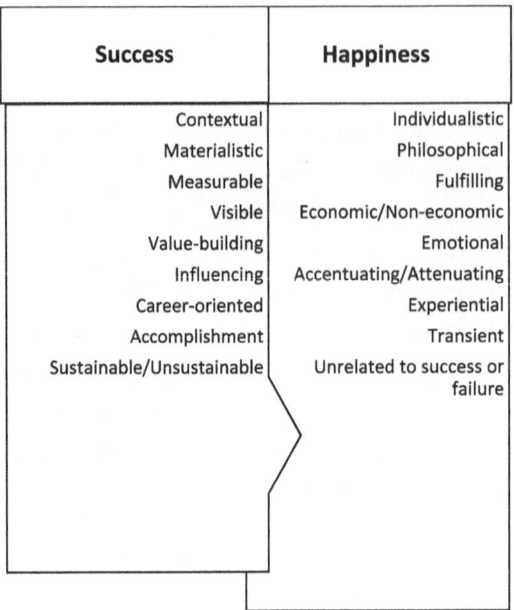

Figure 30.1: Characteristics of Success and Happiness

Convergence Within Divergence

Success and happiness, though correlated with success being the independent variable and happiness being the dependent variable, are not necessarily convergent phenomena. A baby instantly derives happiness upon achieving the success of cuddle from the mother. A child derives success when he or she accomplishes a mechanistic activity, seen to be beyond reach, and in the process of performance also derives much happiness. However, as the child grows into a student and as a student becomes an employee, what determines success and how it influences happiness become divergent and individualized. The goal of progressive organizations, not unnaturally, is to set up people for success to make them happy and also to have happy people in the organization so that the firm can be positioned for success.

It is up to the individuals to recognize that it is important for their lives to seek the convergence of success and happiness. It is up to the organizations to facilitate a nexus between happiness and success by celebrating success. However, it is important for both the individuals and the organizations to build a culture of an organization that facilitates the convergence of success and happiness even though divergent parameters define and drive each outcome of success and happiness. This would be possible when individuals and organizations understand two fundamental concepts of integrating success and happiness. These are awareness management and resilience management. These two concepts are grounded on the premise that neither success nor happiness is absolute and there exists a large latitude to achieve success even after failure and ensure happiness despite unhappiness.

Awareness Management

When an individual or an organization is asked as to what determines success in an organization, the answer is likely to be that a combination of competencies and attitudes determines the success. While this is true, it is awareness that makes a fundamental difference in influencing success or failure. Awareness itself has two facets: internal and external. Internal or self-awareness enables one to appreciate one's competencies and attitudes, delineating adequacies, and inadequacies in each. In an organizational context, it is not unusual for employees to have varied competencies and attitudes. Self-awareness enables an employee to play to his or her strengths rather than follow stereotypes of performance or just stick to assigned roles despite the misalignment. Self-examination is psychologically nuanced and requires that one honestly challenges one's beliefs and marshals the courage to act on information that may lead to fresh ways of thinking about one's life and on what determines one's successes and happiness.

The theory of Argyris and Schon (1978) points out the value of learning through awareness approaches. When an error is detected and corrected but permits the organization to carry on its present policies or achieve its present objectives, then that error-and-correction process is single-loop learning. Single-loop learning is like a thermostat that learns when it is too hot or too cold and turns the heat on or off accordingly. The thermostat can perform this task because it can receive information (the temperature of the room) and take corrective action. Double-loop learning occurs when an error is detected and corrected in ways that involve the modification of an organization's underlying norms, policies, and objectives. Employees who follow the double-loop learning process are able to appreciate where and how their competencies and attitudes align with organizational roles and responsibilities. Organizations that follow double-loop learning are able to induct and develop talent that meets higher aspirations. Clearly, organizations must also deploy double-loop learning, which together with employees' own approach leads to synergistic results.

External awareness deploys double loop learning with an additional strategic context. An individual should not be content with one's own awareness but should seek 360-degree feedback on what others perceive of him or her. He or she also should resort to established psychological analytical tools to understand one's own self better. An organization must similarly look at successful organizations and try to understand what makes them more successful or less successful and more vibrant or less vibrant than itself, with the level of vibrancy setting the organizational tone of happiness. While awareness of an individual is hampered by one's relative ego state or closed state of mind, awareness of an organization is limited by the relative bureaucracy and ossification in its management. Managing for awareness, both internal and external, is a key facet of an individual's and organization's success factors. A cognitive approach that questions every aspect of competencies and attitudes in relation to internal culture and external environment is helpful for both individuals and organizations. Figure 30.2 illustrates single-loop and double-loop learning.

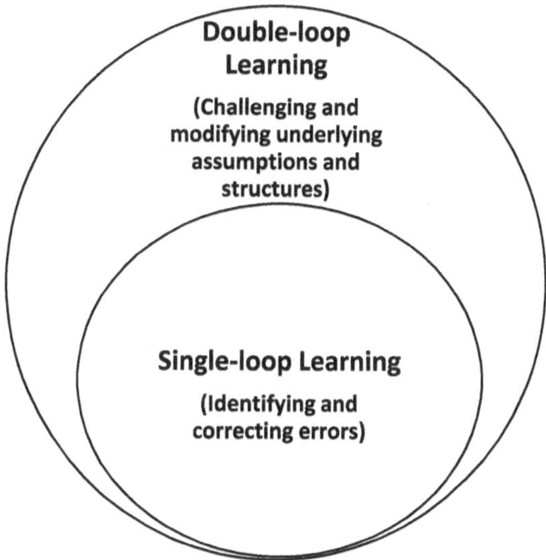

Figure 30.2: Single-loop and Double-loop Learning

Resilience Management

Resilience in terms of physics is the ability of a substance to return to its original shape after it has been bent, stretched, or pressed. In a people sense, it is the ability of people or organizations to feel better quickly and recover appropriately after the occurrence of anything unpleasant or unexpected, such as shock and injury. Resilience is also an age-related phenomenon. As we know, toddlers, infants, and youngsters have tremendous resilience in their skeletal and muscular systems that inevitably decline over age. Gymnasts and sports persons sustain or even improve resilience by adopting exacting training and skilful techniques, along with an openness to take risks. Brain development stops at a particular young age and declines at the old age; one requires specific efforts at improving brain plasticity to maintain the best possible brain function. Organizations also tend to display a lowering resilience with age. Start-ups and young firms typically are able to have flexibility, adaptability, and agility. Such firms return to the growth path quickly despite setbacks. Mature firms, in contrast, tend to be non-resilient.

Resilience in an individual and organizational context has deeper import. Given the unpredictable external environment and heightened competition on one hand and periodical assessments of employees' performance by the managements and quarterly evaluations of the firm's performance by investors on the other hand, performance shocks and unpleasant feedback are commonplace. In respect of individuals, resilience is the ability to withstand shocks, stabilize one's mind and heart, and reevaluate one's competencies and attitudes in the perspective of a long career of four decades. In respect of organizations, resilience is the ability to take performance and competitive setbacks in stride, update strategy and tactics, reinforce and motivate the talent base, and create a new energy. Firms will do well to remember that unlike individuals, they can be ageless if they are resilient (apart from being aware).

Importantly, being resilient is different from being fatalistic. The outstanding example of resilience is that of Japan, a country that virtually rose from ashes after World War II to become the world's leading technological and economic power. The resilience of Japan has been a resultant of the brain power and the work ethic of the people. Individuals and firms need to marshal the hidden brain power and the ignored work ethic to develop a customized hypothesis of resilience. Knee-jerk or ad-hoc responses hamper rather than reinforce the resilience of individuals as much as of corporations. Individuals may have different response mechanisms and abilities to reinforce resilience; for example, silence and pause could give the mind and the heart a chance to recoup the innate optimism and energy. Organizations may also have different response mechanisms and abilities to reinforce resilience; for example, reviews, collaboration, and networking may help the firm to emerge stronger.

The foregoing brings out that awareness management and resilience management have a major role to play in ensuring the success and happiness of individuals as well as of organizations. Certainly, talent and dedication (as well as luck) play crucial roles in success, but one needs to be aware of one's own competencies and attitudes in relation to what is required in the context of internal and external requirements. Despite the right talent and attitudes, individuals and organizations do face setbacks due to several internal and external factors. Resilience with persistence marks the difference between leaders and followers. Awareness and Resilience together typically arm individuals and organizations to derive sustained success and happiness, despite there being no universally applicable benchmarks of success and happiness.

Bibliography

Arbinger Institute. "Humility is a Radical Self-Awareness," *Arbinger Institute,* November 1, 2017.

Argyris, C., & Schon, D. Organizational learning: A theory of action perspective. Reading, MA: Addison-Wesley, 1978.

Barsade, Sigal, and Olivia A. O'Neill. "Manage Your Emotional Culture," *Harvard Business Review* – Leadership and Managing People, January–February 2016.

Bhaktavatsala Rao, C. "Legendary Leaders: Insights and Lessons," Notion Press, 2023.

Bhaktavatsala Rao, C. "Dharmic Management: Lessons from the Indian Social Ecosystem," Notion Press, 2023.

Diane Coutu. "How Resilience Works?" *Harvard Business Review* – Organizational Structure," May 2002.

Erus Angelo A. Lumague. "Relative Value of Hard Skills and Soft Skills for Hiring Employees in Manufacturing Sector," *Journal of Business and Management Studies*, April 2017, Vol. 3, Issue 1, pp. 1–5.

George, Jennifer M. "Emotions and Leadership: The Role of Emotional Intelligence," *Human Relations*, 2000, Vol. 53, Issue 8, pp. 1027–1055.

Henrich R. Greve. "Organizational Learning and Adaptation," Oxford Research Encyclopedia of Business and Management, March 2017.

Jim Whitehurst. "Leaders Can Shape Company Culture through Their Behaviors," *Harvard Business Review* – Leadership, October 13, 2016.

Leigh, Buchanan, and Andrew O'Connell. "A Brief History of Decision Making," *Harvard Business Review* – Organizational Culture, January 2006.

Lerner, Jennifer S., Ye Li, Piercarlo Valdesolo, and Karim Kassam. "Emotion and Decision Making," *Annual Review of Psychology*, June 16, 2014.

Michael R. Wade, and Andrew Tarling. "Humility in Learning: The Surprising Leadership Capability for a Digital Age," IMD – International Institute for Management Development, 2017.

Mineo, D.L. "The Importance of Trust in Leadership," *Research Management Review*, 2014, Vol. 20.

Namrata Singh. "Humility makes CEOs from India Stand Out," Times of India, May 9, 2014

Nyameh Jerome. "Application of the Maslow's Hierarchy of Need Theory; Impacts and Implications on Organizational Culture, Human Resource and Employee's Performance," *International Journal of Business and Management Invention*, March 2013, Vol. 2, Issue 3, pp. 39–45.

Owens, Bradley P., Michael D. Johnson, and Terence R. Mitchell. "Expressed Humility in Organizations: Implications for Performance, Teams and Leadership," *Organization Science,* October 25, 2013, Vol. 24, Issue 5, pp. 1517–1538.

People Matters. “Who’s Better: A Task-Oriented Leader or a People-Oriented Leader?” *Employee Engagement*, June 6, 2016.

Rao, C. B. “Leadership for India Inc.: An Experiential Treatise,” Notion Press, 2017.

Savani, Krishna, Siran Zhan, and Christina Fang. “A Behavioral Decision Making Perspective on Organizational Inefficiencies,” *Academy of Management Proceedings*, January 2017.

Savani, Krishna, Siran Zhan, and Christina Fang. “A Behavioral Decision Making Perspective on Organizational Inefficiencies,” *Academy of Management – Proceedings*, January 2017.

Sikora, David M., and Gerald R. Ferris. “Strategic Human Resource Practice Implementation: The Critical Role of Management,” Most Cited Human Resource Management Review Articles – Scopus, Elsevier, January 2014, Vol. 24, Issue 3, pp. 271–281.

Soldz, Stephen, and George E. Vaillant. “The Big Five Personality Traits and the Life Course: A 45-Year Longitudinal Study,” *Journal of Research in Personality*, 1999, Vol. 33, pp. 208–232.

Spender. J. “Making Knowledge the Basis of a Dynamic Theory of the Firm,” *Strategic Management Journal*, 1996, Vol. 17, pp. 45–62.

Srivastava, Kalpana. “Emotional Intelligence and Organizational Effectiveness,” *Industry Psychiatry Journal*, July–December 2013, Vol. 22, Issue 2, pp. 97–99.

Steel P. “The Nature of Procrastination: A Meta-Analytic and Theoretical Review of Quintessential Self-Regulatory

Failure," *Psychological Bulletin*, 2007, Vol. 133, Issue 1, pp. 65–94.

Suar, Damodar, and Rooplekha Khuntia. "Does Ethical Climate Influence Unethical Practices and Work Behavior?" *Journal of Human Values*, April 1, 2004, Vol. 10, Issue 1, pp. 11–21.

Sulaiman, Che Noraiani., Hashim, Mohamed Burhan Ibrahim, and Sumantra Ghoshal. "Bad Management Theories are Destroying Good Management Practices," Academy of Management Learning and Education, March 1, 2005, Vol.4, Issue 1, pp. 75–91.

Sweta Rajan-Rankin. "Self-Identity, Embodiment and the Development of Emotional Resilience," *British Journal of Social Work*, 2014, Vol. 44, pp. 2426–2442.

Tarique, Ibraiz, and Randall S. Schuler. "Global Talent Management: Literature review, Integrative framework, and Suggestions for Further Research," *Journal of World Business*, 2010, Vol. 45, pp. 122–133.

Tewari, Ruchi, and Ritu Sharma. "Hard Skills Vs Soft Skills: A Co-Relational Study," Research Gate, Article, June 2010.

Therasa, Chandrasekar, and Chidambaram Vijayabanu. "The Impact of Big Five Personality Traits and Positive Psychological Strengths towards Job Satisfaction: a Review," *Periodica Polytechnica Social and Management Sciences*, December 2, 2014.

The Art of Living Foundation. "The Benefits of Meditation."

http://www.artofliving.org/meditation/meditation-for-you/benefitsof-meditation.

The Organization for Economic Co-operation and Development (OECD). "Competency Framework," Talent OECD, November 2014.

Torres, Christine. "Humility's Role in Leadership," *The Journal of Healthcare Contracting*, November 8, 2017.

Tripathi, Kaushiki, Manisha Agrawal. "Competency Based Management in Organizational Context: A Literature Review," *Global Journal of Finance and Management*, 2014, Vol. 6, Issue 4, pp. 349–356.

Tsai, Yafang. "Relationship between Organizational Culture, Leadership Behavior and Job Satisfaction," Tsai BMC Health Services Research, 2011, Vol. 11, Issue 98.

Wang, Y., and Tzyy-Ping Jung. "A Collaborative Brain-Computer Interface for Improving Human Performance," *PLoS ONE*, May 31, 2011, Vol. 6, Issue 5.

About the Author

Dr. C. Bhaktavatsala Rao received his Ph.D. Degree in Industrial Management and M. Tech. Degree in Industrial Engineering from the Indian Institute of Technology Madras, Chennai. He received his B.E. Degree in Mechanical Engineering from Sri Venkateswara University, Tirupati.

Dr. C. B. Rao has over forty-nine years of diversified experience in strategic and operational leadership of large, reputed companies, including global multinational corporations, in India. Dr. C. B. Rao's last formal assignment was as Managing Director/Executive Chairman of Hospira Healthcare India Pvt Limited, a Pfizer Company. Dr. Rao is a prolific writer with several publications in economic and business dailies and refereed journals. Dr Rao is the founder of LeaderCrest Academy. This book is the fourteenth in the series of books authored and published by Dr. Rao under his LeaderCrest Banner over the last six years.

Dr. C. B. Rao serves as Ajit Singhvi Chair Professor in the Department of Management Studies, Indian Institute of Technology Madras, Chennai. He serves as non-executive director on the boards of select companies. He also serves as adviser to global corporations.

www.ingramcontent.com/pod-product-compliance
Lightning Source LLC
LaVergne TN
LVHW041154150826
845673LV00001B/157

* 9 7 9 8 8 9 1 3 3 3 5 9 8 *